INCESSANT DRUMBEAT

TRIAL AND TRIUMPH IN IRIAN JAYA

INCESSANT DRUMBEAT

TRIAL AND TRIUMPH IN IRIAN JAYA

by
Mary Beth Lagerborg

CHRISTIAN • LITERATURE • CRUSADE
Fort Washington, Pennsylvania 19034

CHRISTIAN LITERATURE CRUSADE

U.S.A.
P.O. Box 1449, Fort Washington, PA 19034

BRITAIN
51 The Dean, Alresford, Hants SO24 9BJ

AUSTRALIA
P.O. Box 91, Pennant Hills N.S.W. 2120

NEW ZEALAND
P.O. Box 1203, Palmerston North

Photo Credits
All photographs unless otherwise marked are from the
Rascher Family Album

ISBN 0-87508-968-2

Cover photo: Superstock, Inc.

PRINTED IN THE UNITED STATES OF AMERICA

CONTENTS

Therefore, my dear brothers,
stand firm.
Let nothing move you.
Always give yourselves fully
to the work of the Lord,
because you know
that your labor in the Lord
is not in vain.

I Corinthians 15:58, NIV

FOREWORD

My friend Larry Rascher has more in common with the Apostle Paul than any other man I know. For a start, Paul of Tarsus was extremely *mobile* as an ambassador for Christ. Willing to preach Christ anywhere, Paul sought especially to preach Him where He had not yet been proclaimed. He feared lest he underemploy the Holy Spirit's gifts by building on old foundations, instead of pouring new ones. Thus, after he had engospeled an 1800–mile–long arc reaching from Jerusalem to Illyria [Yugoslavia], Paul set out for Rome and Spain!

The same spirit led Larry of St. Louis to serve on at least four formidable frontiers in Irian Jaya.

Paul said that he had been "exposed to death again and again . . . shipwrecked . . . spent a night and a day in the open sea . . . in danger from rivers . . . from bandits." He added: "I have labored and toiled and often gone without sleep; I have known hunger and thirst. . . . Besides everything else, I face daily the pressure of my concern for all the churches" (II Cor. 11: 23–28, *NIV*).

If asked to name which of these trials he too has experienced, Larry Rascher could reply, "All of the above."

There is still another parallel: Paul of Tarsus employed a secular talent along with his spiritual gifts. He made tents. Larry, a journeyman carpenter, left a virtual *town* consisting of a well–constructed hospital, schools, clinics, airstrips, and missionary dwellings in the wake of his travels across Irian Jaya.

Paul not only went and preached; he also returned and wrote letters—the Pauline epistles—inspiring successive waves of frontier–crossers ever since to follow his example. Larry has emulated this aspect of Paul's labor as well. *Incessant Drumbeat* is a Rascheresque epistle. Some who read it may wish that its publisher had printed a warning on the cover. It would say: "Some material may not be suitable for the weak–hearted or the self–centered. Read at the risk of the complacency you may or may not know you have."

Beyond these and other comparisons I do however note a startling contrast. Paul endured shipwreck, grief and trial as a *single* man. Larry had his wife beside him all the way! Thus what follows is much more than the story of a rugged man. It is also the story of a woman of rarest quality. A woman named Shirley.

To the eye, Shirley appears so fragile one would think the mere *threat* of suffering, let alone suffering in reality, would send her flying like a leaf in the wind. Not so. The love of Christ, combined with the gentle, open–hearted love she and Larry share, has given Shirley Rascher an inner strength most men three times her size might envy. The Rascher children also reflect that heritage of strong love.

Ah, they are much more than mere *survivors*, these Raschers. God's grace has made them *surmounters!*

Don Richardson

PART ONE

THE SOUTH COAST

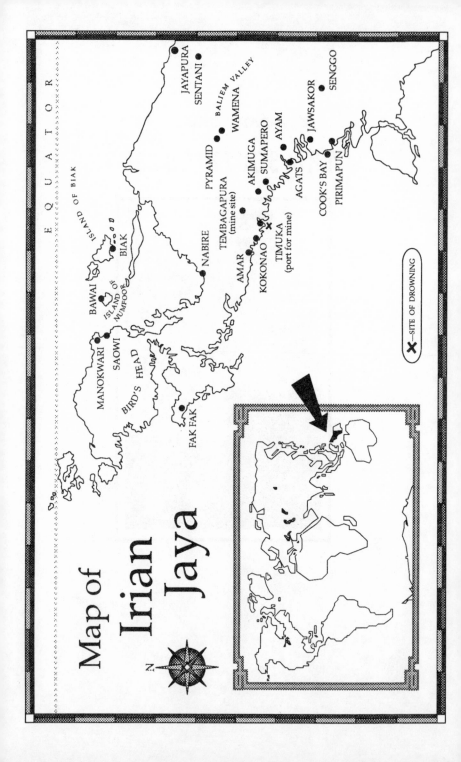

CALLED TO THE COASTLANDS

Larry sat atop the cabin of his twenty-six foot motor boat, the Ebenezer. Through a hole in the front of the cabin roof he could work the steering wheel below with his feet. His eyes scanned the river for submerged trees and floating logs. The boat rocked gently in the turbid waters of the vast swamps of West Irian's south coast. Larry swatted at sand flies that tickled his neck just above his T-shirt. He was glad to be on the river again, to be back among the Nafaripi instead of building houses in Michigan. Larry smiled to himself as he navigated.

Larry and Shirley Rascher were just back from furlough. The church in Kokonao had invited Larry to preach and then to visit awhile. It was a journey of one hundred twenty-five miles by water from Sumapero, where they lived with the Nafaripi tribe, to Kokonao.

Larry had brought Moses with them. Moses was a tall, strong national, long on ability and loyalty. Larry usually knew the rivers, which were constantly changing with the tides, but Moses always did.

"Hey, Lawrence, want a helper?" Shirley stood on the deck of the boat below him holding two-and-a-half-year-old Karen. "Gregory's helping me cook supper, and I thought you might need a helper, too."

"Come on up here, Karen." He swung her up easily with

one arm. She was a tiny wisp in a sunsuit and sandals. Her fine light-brown hair was kept short because of the heat. Her little face was all hazel eyes, full of wonder. Larry sat her between his legs. She chattered contentedly from this high-up look at the watery world, pointing out metalic-blue butterflies and parrots in the sago palms and the mangrove thickets. Soon they were singing together.

Behind the Ebenezer's small enclosed cabin was its two-cylinder diesel engine and then a sixteen-foot-long plywood canopy with canvas side curtains. Here Shirley had set up the kitchen. She was steaming rice in a pot while Greg, who was nearly four, cut up a papaya. Odd-shaped pieces kept slipping into his mouth. "That's enough, Greg."

"Can I give some to my Karen?" he asked. The two looked out for each other.

"She'll be down in a bit for supper." Shirley lifted the lid from the pot of rice and added some cooked chicken from one Tupperware container and sauce from another. Shirley had gained a little weight and regained good health during her year in the U.S. Fellow missionaries on the field said they had never seen her look prettier.

Shirley watched Greg and wiped the perspiration from her forehead. She missed her helper and companion, fourteen-year-old Kathy. Twins Keith and Kathy, the oldest of their five children, had flown to Manila to Faith Academy to start high school two weeks before.

Rain came without warning, in pounding sheets, and drove them all under the canopy for supper.

Chip Rascher was eleven. His head and heart were full of *Robinson Crusoe* and *Swiss Family Robinson*. This trip was to be a golden adventure before he was off to boarding school in Sentani. This first night out he was too excited to settle in and suggested they all go fishing. They dropped anchor. There was little moon and they couldn't navigate the tangle of rivers in the darkness and steady rain.

Shirley lit a Coleman lantern and held it on the side of the boat. As Greg and Karen peered over the edge, schools of small fish were drawn to the lantern like June bugs to a porch light. Chip, Moses and Larry worked their way along the side of the boat with ten-foot bamboo poles fitted with gigs. They speared several of the little fish to use as bait.

Greg tried to hold the slippery fish in his pudgy hands. Fishing lines with hooks and weights were tied on each side of the boat and a couple off the stern. Greg helped bait the lines. Within a couple of hours they had caught six catfish for breakfast.

Shirley enjoyed watching her family in the lantern light. In the States on furlough she had missed the good family times around the lantern in Sumapero. She thought of Jesus Christ, Light of the World. She hoped He radiated from their lives in this land where the people lived in bondage to evil spirits, spells and rituals of revenge.

The missionaries in West Irian were keenly aware of the spiritual warfare engulfing them—and its consequences. A search was then underway for a Mission Aviation Fellowship pilot who had gone down with his plane. Another pilot, who would have flown the Raschers to Kokonao, was down with a strange virus which had left him temporarily without the use of his arms.

On this particular trip the Raschers were glad to be out on the Ebenezer. Larry had purchased the boat just before furlough from its maker, John McCain, a missionary in West Irian with the Regions Beyond Missionary Union. The Ebenezer had a plywood hull. It was quite seaworthy and would be a great help in the work of TEAM missionaries along the south coast. A trip by boat was less costly than an MAF flight and more supplies could be hauled in one load. And boating was part of the fun of missionary life.

That night Shirley slept in the cramped cabin with Karen and Greg on beds that folded down from the side walls. The others slept under the canopy with more breeze and mosquitoes.

The next day Larry hoped to make up some time. They traveled perhaps seventy-five miles. Moses took turns steering, as did Chip any chance he got. Greg and Karen played on the boat and asked several times when they were going to get there.

They turned into one river which took them to a mucky dead end, causing a three hour delay. Larry was now concerned about fuel. They couldn't afford to waste any more.

A huge crocodile rolled off the bank and glided along-side the boat. Moses gave Chip the wheel and grabbed the crocodile spear. Larry pulled out the super-8mm camera in time to trace the arc of the spear through the air, aimed for the soft spot behind the croc's head. The spear tip lit on top of his head, bent, and glanced off. The croc rolled over, kicked up spray and swam away. "We didn't give him much more than a good headache," Larry chuckled. They had missed a good meal of the fillet behind the croc's back legs.

Later in the day they passed a crocodile hunter from Kokonao in his dugout canoe. Larry killed the motor and they drifted, talking for a while. The hunter had come a distance on the ocean rather than taking the all-river route from Kokonao. "The ocean in the morning was smooth like glass," he said.

Larry had planned to follow the rivers. All their life jackets were packed in their outfit which hadn't arrived yet from the States. But he began to consider going by ocean to a river mouth that would take them into Kokonao by a much shorter route. It could save four hours travel time and conserve fuel. They had traveled to Kokonao by ocean many times before in boats far inferior to the Ebenezer.

Before nightfall they dropped anchor at the mouth of the Koperapoka River and watched the sun set over the ocean. No one was hungry for supper so they didn't bother with it. Later Shirley roasted peanuts as they lounged under the canopy.

"Moses, how do you think you'd like peanut butter on your sago?" Larry asked.

"What is peanut butter?" Moses replied.

"Shirley, do you have some peanut butter here for this man to try?" Chip knew she did. They ate lots of it.

"You'd better like it, Moses," said Chip as Shirley spread some on a piece of bread. "You're going to be making enough of it to feed New Guinea." Moses took a tentative bite, then used a long finger to pry it from the roof of his mouth. He smiled, realizing everyone was watching him, but made no comment.

"On furlough I found a peanut grinder and rigged it with a ten horsepower Kohler engine so we can run it without electricity. I got a big roaster, too, out of a restaurant," Larry said.

Seeing that Moses was finishing his piece of bread, Shirley spread him another one. "Larry used to lie awake at night in Sumapero thinking of this," she added.

"Peanuts will grow in salt water and I figure the Nafaripi can grow them right in Sumapero." Larry's voice grew louder with excitement. "The peanuts will give them protein. We can roast the peanuts, grind them, mix them with a little coconut oil, and have a product to trade at the *tokos* in Kokonao. You can grow peanuts in Wapu, too, and bring them to Sumapero for processing."

Moses didn't know whether they were joking or serious, so he looked from one to another for a clue.

"No kiddin', Moses. You should see the size of this grinder!" Chip said.

"I'm waiting to hear what the pilots say when these

things show up at the MAF base in Sentani. The grinder alone will be two plane loads." Shirley laughed at her husband, who had a reputation among the missionaries for crazy ideas. She knew he sincerely wanted to make life better for the nationals. The other missionaries teased Larry, but they loved having him around.

Saturday morning they all rose early. They prayed together, committing the day to the Lord. Larry had conferred with Moses and Chip and decided to take the ocean. They started out by 7:00 a.m., figuring they would eat breakfast when they were well underway. They would follow the coastline to the second river mouth to the west, there enter the Tipuka River, and be in Kokonao by noon. The Tipuka River mouth was used by boats servicing a large American copper mine in the mountains above it. It was wide and well marked with buoys.

To the west was blue sky. To the east clouds threatened rain, which tended to calm the sea. The tide was just beginning to come in. At low tide the south coast is mud flats extending out many miles. The Ebenezer made its way ten miles into the ocean to deeper water and then turned west to follow the shoreline, which was still in view. The sea was a bit choppy. The breeze was from the south, which usually portended calm seas.

The Raschers received a newspaper clipping months later from a friend in Oxford, Michigan. On July twenty-third an earthquake at sea between Australia and New Guinea registering 6.5 triggered rough seas across 500 miles in twenty-four hours. This was the morning of July 24, 1971.

This family aboard the Ebenezer had come far in miles of life. They were so young when the journey began.

There might as well have been a brass band the morning the Maplewood Congregational Church of St. Louis, Missouri, sent them as its missionaries to a primitive field in June of 1961. Two hundred friends, relatives and church members crowded the TWA boarding area. Flight attendants were not yet used to crowds. They treated the boarding family royally.

The pastor prayed. Then en masse the flock proceeded down the steps and onto the ramp. The intrepid missionary family climbed the airstairs toward the open hatch of the 727. It took a while. Larry Rascher carried eighteen-month-old Paul, or "Chipper." He turned around, waved, and grinned as he waited for his wife Shirley to ascend with their three-year-old twins, Keith and Kathy, on either hand. They looked like any young American family struggling into an aircraft.

The family settled into their seats, passing restless Chipper from lap to lap. Shirley examined the new disposable diapers that TWA provided for the flight. "Lawrence, look at this," she laughed. "They're no thicker than Kleenex!"

Shirley figured she had in her flight bag what the children would need for the many hours on the airplane. And if she didn't, she thought, they would get by. Shirley removed her hat. She had a fresh permanent, her blond hair cut short to be manageable.

The children were blond and hazel-eyed. And they were extremely curious about the seat pockets, the tray tables and the arriving planes visible out the little square windows.

Larry was a journeyman carpenter and a graduate of Columbia Bible College. His dark hair was in a crew cut for life in the tropics. He had given away his white buck shoes, which he wouldn't need in Netherlands New Guinea. Larry would be a missionary builder for The Evangelical Alliance Mission (TEAM).

Shirley grew up in St. Louis, the youngest of ten children. Her dad had liked to load the kids into the back of his pickup truck and park close to the airport to watch the planes arrive and depart. Now Shirley was flying for the first time, and to the far side of the world. Her dad had died some time ago, and it was hard to say goodbye to her mom.

Larry's mother had died of a cerebral hemorrhage when Larry was in high school. His father, a contractor, would have loved for Larry to build with him in St. Louis. Larry hated to leave his dad and the Cardinals and baseball.

But the work ahead of them exerted an unrelenting pull. They had prepared for it through college, a missionary internship, the Summer Institute of Linguistics, and ordination. They had the prayers and financial support of a cluster of small-town churches in Michigan, where they had been living, as well as from Maplewood Congregational of St. Louis.

In the fall of 1952, Larry's freshman year, Netherlands New Guinea moved from oblivion to preoccupation in the minds of the students of Columbia Bible College. Word came from the State Department that Walter Erickson and Edward Tritt, both graduates of CBC, had been murdered by their native carriers. They had been on a trek to open missionary work for TEAM to primitive tribes in the Bird's Head area of Netherlands New Guinea.

In a moving memorial service at the school, approximately twenty students rose to say that they would pray about the possibility of taking the men's places. Larry hadn't known the men and didn't stand, but he was moved to begin attending the Southeast Asia prayer group and to pray for the Lord's work in New Guinea.

During Larry's senior year at CBC his favorite class was Progress of Redemption, taught by Buck Hatch.

The main point of the class—in Larry's view, anyway—was that God was moving toward a goal: that people from every tribe and nation would one day make up the body of Christ in heaven. Hatch taught that Jesus Christ would not return to earth until this mission was accomplished. Larry took from the class an urgency to reach isolated tribes with the gospel.

A chapel missionary speaker expounded on the same subject. Larry questioned him.

"I'm not inferring that God loves some people more than others. We're not called to make everyone Christians, but to call out some from every tribe and nation," he replied.

The cumulative effect was a desire on Larry's part to go with the gospel to primitive tribes in Netherlands New Guinea. But how could he know for certain that such an undertaking was the Lord's will for him? Friends prayed with him in the Southeast Asia prayer group. Larry was reading the Bible cover to cover, as was required of CBC students, and asking God to speak to him about the matter through its pages. The answer came to him insistently through many verses in the book of Isaiah, verses which Larry underlined in his college study Bible, such as

> *Sing to the Lord a new song,*
> *Sing His praise from the end of the earth!*
> *You who go down to the sea, and all that is in it,*
> *You islands and those who dwell on them. . . .*
> *Let them give glory to the Lord,*
> *And declare His praise in the coastlands.*
> *Isaiah 42:10,12, NAS*

Did the call include Shirley Ray? Larry was in love with Shirley, and asked the Lord for guidance in their relationship. After a series of verses had given him the assurance he needed, Larry pasted a picture of Shirley on the front page of his Bible. Next to it he wrote the following: "Lord, wanting the will of God more than anything else in the world and knowing that Thou dost know what's best for me, I stand for the rest of my life on the basis of all I know and can know, that it is Thy will to make Shirley and I one. Thank you, Father." They were married soon after Larry's graduation in 1956.

Now they brought three children with them across the world. As their flight out of Los Angeles crossed the Pacific, Keith and Kathy slept on the floor in front of them, in the extra legroom of their front-row seats. Chip was curled in Shirley's lap.

Larry's childhood memories were of uncomplicated weekends hunting squirrels and rabbits with his dad and his twin brother, Leonard, or fishing the Meramec River together. What would life hold for these children in such a strange land? Would they find friends to play with? Would they stay healthy? Would they adjust to boarding school? Could Larry and Shirley even let them go to boarding school? They were confident that the Lord had called them. Consequently, this was the life He had in mind for their children as well. He would go with them and bless them. But would it mean sacrifices on the children's part?

They talked as seriously about life in New Guinea as a couple can who are young, hopeful, in love and eager to begin their lifework. They well knew the story of martyrs Erickson and Tritt. They knew, too, that Shirley had allergies and sometimes fragile health. But New Guinea was where God wanted them to be. If they were to die there, they agreed, so be it.

They were all in this adventure together. A circle bound them close in the darkened plane, in the night over the Atlantic. Out the window the big dipper seemed to be pouring out into the cup which was theirs. He who created the stars was enfolding them and carrying them into a dark land.

NETHERLANDS NEW GUINEA

New Guinea, the earth's second largest island, spreads like a flying turkey in the South Pacific, north of Australia. It is the easternmost of the Spice Islands, the tip of the Malay Archipelago, the eastern end of today's Indonesia. Its topography is so rugged and impenetrable that time and exploration long avoided it.

Along its spine run mountain ranges rearing from sea level to 16,550 feet, cut by deep gorges and turbulent rivers.

The south coast of New Guinea is the world's largest swamp, a land without boundaries. Rivers run through it like capillaries at ebb tide. At flood tide the rivers deepen and many of them merge. Between the rivers are mangrove thickets, jungle, and mud.

Lying just below the equator, New Guinea's climate is a daily 90° Fahrenheit with about equal percent humidity, except when it rains (as it does most days), and except in the interior highlands, where it is cooler and even wetter.

The Dutch East India Company claimed the western half of the island in 1660. They weren't interested in the place, but they wanted to prevent other countries from gaining a toehold of trade in their fabulous Dutch East India empire. In 1828, the Netherlands made a formal claim to sovereignty and established a token settlement on the island. The eastern half of the island, claimed by Great Britain, later came under the jurisdiction of Australia. It was eventually given independence as Papua New Guinea, which means Island of the Fuzzy-Hairs in Malay (Indonesian), the local trade language.

Native to New Guinea is a Melanesian race of people with bushy black hair and dark skin. They are isolated by the terrain into tribal groups, each with its own language or dialect—hundreds of them—and each tribe numbering from tens to perhaps 75,000. The heartier, larger tribes populate the interior highlands and the north coast. Sparcer tribes survive as they can, usually as nomadic food gatherers, in the miasmic, malaria-ridden south coast swamps.

The natives are animists, trying by spells and fetishes to placate the spirit world which somehow controls at whim whether their crops grow or their children live. Revenge, intertribal warfare, witchcraft, head-hunting and cannibalism were commonplace. It is not a place one would choose to raise children. Its climate, culture, topography, and the illiteracy and multiplicity of languages have formed strong barriers against survival, much less the communication of a new way of thought and life.

The Dutch had established clean, orderly settlements in a few large coastal villages, but had largely ignored the hostile tribes and terrain of the south coast swamps and the interior.

Even today, no one except an archaeologist, a well-paid mining engineer, a vagabond adventurer or a transmigrated Indonesian would journey to Netherlands New Guinea—later West Irian and now Irian Jaya—unless impelled by a great cause. Larry and Shirley Rascher were impelled to these wilds by the living God.

The Rascher family was dressed up, Larry in a suit and tie, Shirley in a cotton dress, the children in

Sunday best when they disembarked in Manokwari, Netherlands New Guinea. In a sense New Guinea was dressed for the occasion as well. Manokwari, a major Dutch village on the north coast, was its jewel. Its fine deep harbor was rimmed by verdant jungle-carpeted mountains. Trim Dutch houses and *tokos*—small shops run by Chinese or Dutch merchants—lined the dirt roads. Native villages rambled on stilts along the coastline in either direction. Out in the bay natives spearfished from outrigger canoes, while on the beaches naked black children poked in the sand for crabs.

It was not a bad place to await assignment and to adjust to life in the tropics. The Raschers were met at the airport by some fellow TEAM missionaries and were taken by a vehicle that was half-car, half-truck— two back seats with a canopy—to the neighboring village of Saowi. At the rare sound of an approaching automobile, native children ran to the road waving: *"Dah! Dah!"* The little Raschers were entranced with the native children and the human traffic walking or riding bicycles along the narrow roads.

The Erickson-Tritt Bible Institute which was their destination in Saowi consisted of three missionary dwellings, a storage house, and one school/dormitory building for its thirty male students.

Here the family settled into a corrugated aluminum house which Shirley called "the hot house." They awaited the annual conference in August of all TEAM missionaries in Netherlands New Guinea.

As the days passed, they became used to the thick, wet heat which slowed them during the day and left them tossing on a sheet at night, and to the insects which doggedly invaded food of any sort. Fellow missionaries taught them how to shop in the markets and *tokos*. Shirley learned to cook meals on one burner and to manage native house helpers.

Larry helped with fix-up tasks around the school and played soccer with the Bible school boys, with whom he first employed his unconscious philosophy of communication: If you don't speak their language, talk louder.

The possibilities of location for their assignment were shaped by an agreement between the missions on the island. For many years Roman Catholic missions had operated on the south coast and the Dutch Reformed Church on the north coast. In addition, various evangelical Protestant missions had divided the island into mission territories. This spread the work more effectively and avoided duplication of effort and possible conflict. TEAM had assumed responsibility for the northeastern tip or Bird's Head of the island and the swamplands of the south coast. The mission's field office was in Manokwari.

The various Protestant missions joined in what they called TMF—The Mission Fellowship. Much united them: the isolation and dangers of work in primitive areas, the need to present a united front in dealing with the encroaching Indonesian government, and Christian love and concern for one another. TMF collectively built a warehouse on the north coast in Sentani through which missionaries could buy precious canned foods from Australia, the Netherlands and the U.S.A. TMF missionaries helped with the baby-sitting and cooking for one another's annual conferences. Many of them sent their children to a boarding school in Sentani run by the Christian and Missionary Alliance. Most TMF missionary families vacationed in Sentani to be near their children and shop the warehouse. By talking via shortwave radio and by sharing air transportation through Mission Aviation Fellowship (MAF), they kept up on one another and upheld one another with prayer. The bonding among TMF missionaries in the pioneering stage of the work in Netherlands New

Guinea became an example to mission organizations around the world.

A mission's annual conference in Netherlands New Guinea was far more than a time to take care of mission business and hear an inspirational speaker. After the extreme isolation of their daily lives, what missionaries principally came to do was TALK—talk and laugh together over situations they all understood. Life with primitive tribes was so stressful that missionaries learned they could either cry, and eventually fall apart in the crying, or laugh. Laughter was survival.

At their first annual conference the Raschers met the pioneers of TEAM's work on the island. Many of them were the same guys who had stood up during the memorial service for Walter Erickson and Ed Tritt at Columbia Bible College and said "I'll go." A second wave of missionaries was also present, the Rascher family representing the tail end of it.

It was an ordinary-enough looking bunch. Each were intent, committed Christians willing to give up personal comfort and worldly security for the cause of Jesus Christ. Not all of them were polished preachers, adept linguists or leaders. Some were more inventive than others, some more personable, some more self-disciplined or reserved. Yet God would use each one. Several of these early families would still be there thirty years later. Their successes in terms of people won to Christ would not in all cases make impressive statistics. But they were faithful to their calling, and in those days missionary service was assumed to be long term.

Larry and Shirley were eager to begin their work bringing the gospel to a primitive tribe. They were young and still forming their expectations of what home and work life should be. If Shirley had to step over a snake taking a bottle to Chip in the night, she could learn to take it in stride.

Their first assignment was evangelism among the

Mimika, a predominantly Catholic tribe. They were to settle among them at the Dutch government outpost of Kokonao on the south coast. Harold Lovestrand, who was currently at Kokonao, was a gifted teacher and was badly needed in Saowi at the Bible school. He and his wife would stay on in Kokonao just long enough to teach the Raschers to speak rudimentary Indonesian and help them adjust. Larry would also serve as a builder for TEAM, accepting short-term building assignments anywhere on the island as projects arose.

The Mimika was not an unreached tribe. Their assignment, in fact, was an example of how a mission must often use new recruits to plug the holes created by a veteran missionary leaving the field, for whatever reason. Workers are never as plentiful as the work to be done. Fresh energies are diverted to existing work. True pioneers are few. There are rarely enough missionaries to afford a mission the luxury of planning strategies.

Larry and Shirley settled in Kokonao, willing, yet disappointed.

THE FALSE RELIGION

The village of Kokonao perched along the Mimika River just above where the Mimika emptied into the sea. Kokonoa seemed to be two places. At flood tide murky water swirled up under its houses, which the Dutch built on ironwood pilings. Snakes took refuge in the houses. Garden plots were ravaged, and debris—anything that wasn't tied down—bobbed along the surface. There were no automobiles, no roads, no contact with the outside world except by float plane, radio or boat. Ships brought goods twice a year to Kokonao, but not at flood tide when the ocean was rough. Only the crocodiles, mosquitoes and sand flies liked this melancholy place.

At low tide Kokonao was a travelog beauty. Coconut palms towered over the town in a swaying crown. The Dutch built their homes from *gaba gaba*, the stalks of the sago palm, a clean, tidy, bamboo-like material. The front porches, screened doors and windows invited in breezes. The roofs flared far out past the walls to keep rain out of the windows. Smooth, white sand beaches rather than the usual mud were peculiar to this part of the south coast swamps. The grass around the homes was cut by natives with machetes to keep back the snakes and poisonous lizards. There was no hurry or bustle in Kokonao. People had plenty of time to watch

27

the sunsets, newly painted each evening over a glassy sea.

> And they who dwell in the ends of the earth stand
> in awe of Thy signs;
> Thou dost make the dawn and the sunset shout
> for joy.
>
> Psalm 65:8, NAS

When the Raschers moved to Kokonao, it was a town of 2,500. Most prominent in the community were the government officials and workers who oversaw the Mimika tribe. These were Dutch or natives from tribes which had known civilization long before the Mimika. Many were Biakers from the north coast island of Biak. They were the carpenters, policemen, district officials, agricultural workers, and workmen who built and maintained the boats needed to survey the Mimika tribe.

The Catholic priests in Kokonao were equally important. Nearly all the Mimika children in Kokonao attended the Catholic school. The Catholic complex housed a grammar school, a high school, a Dutch order of priests, a hospital, and a government-approved airstrip. Early in the morning the priests strode back and forth on the airstrip praying, their white robes billowing in the breeze.

Chinese merchants owned the post's two one-room *tokos* —the "old" *toko lama* and the "new" *toko baru.*

The Raschers were not the only Protestants at Kokonao. *Bapak* Humassey, a retired policeman from the neighboring island of Ambon, had begun a small church among the non-Catholic government workers. And TEAM had two representatives there besides the departing Lovestrand family. Doris Florin was a teacher in a one-room Protestant school begun by *Bapak* Humassey, and Phyllis Griffiths was a linguist attempting to translate the Mimika language.

Then there were the Mimika for whom all the others had come. The tribe lived along the rivers many miles on either side of Kokonao. Four clans or villages of them lived on the outskirts of town. Efforts by the Dutch and the priests to improve the lot of the tribe had been accepted to a limited degree. The Dutch had built *gaba gaba* houses for the Mimika, but the Mimikas preferred their own ramshackle huts, which they constructed right behind the government-built houses. Except for the young children, the Mimika were at least partially clothed, providing some protection from the sun and insects. Mimika children were learning to read and write in Indonesian.

The Mimika still used their fetishes, but secretly. Where the men had once worn bones through the septum of their noses, large sagging holes remained. The old initiation rite of filing a boy's teeth to a point had been banned by the Dutch. But the Mimika still practiced this, so young men tried not to smile around whites.

The work of each day for the Mimika consisted of procuring enough food to eat. The women gardened or walked to the ocean to catch shrimp in large oval nets. The men spearfished from their dugout canoes.

The Mimika were known for their carvings: on the tips of their canoes, on spears, and on totem poles along the path to the four tribal villages. Each element of the carvings carried meaning in placating the spirit world: the beak or the eye of a bird, lizards, a long, slender man's face. Nearly everyone carved. But some, the masters, sat under palm-leaf lean-tos, where they could be among the people and feel any stir of breeze as they carved by the hour. Mimikas also gathered under lean-tos to sing.

In the center of Kokonao was a common meeting ground, the soccer field. Kokonao had many soccer teams. The police had a team, as did the Catholic high school, each of the four Mimika clans living at Kokonao, the government workers, and the Protestants.

The children loved to play, and soccer balls were plentiful. The Chinese merchants knew what would sell. There was one additional rule to the game: All players had to either wear shoes or not. When one native village played another they used their wide, flattened, leather-tough feet. The natives were strong and quick and the whites were no match. The natives had time on their hands and loved to play soccer and volleyball.

The Rascher's outfit of household goods arrived load by load in MAF planes. They set up housekeeping in the five-room corrugated aluminum "Lovestrand House." The wood floors were rough but cool. The kitchen was just large enough to hold their Philips kerosene stove, a kerosene refrigerator, and a sink fed from barrels of rainwater collected on a platform at the rear of the house. A cabinet holding their dishes separated the kitchen from the eating area.

In the smallest of the three bedrooms Larry built bunk beds for Keith and Chip. The beds all had foam mattresses and canopies of mosquito netting.

The living room was furnished with rattan furniture and a candy-striped rag rug. They had a stereo and a reel-to-reel tape recorder. Through their open windows their jungle neighbors heard the strange sounds of the gospel music of Gordon Methene (Shirley's favorite), the Blackwood Brothers, Doug Oldham, the Gaithers, and tapes of the Children's Bible Hour from Michigan. A huge black shortwave radio connected them to the larger world. To supplement the town's electric supply, which was sporadic, they used a generator.

A number of sheds and outbuildings enabled the family to function quite efficiently. Under one palm-leaf shed was a wringer-style, gas-operated washing machine. Nearby, a huge copper pot for heating the wash water was set in the top of a metal drum. A long gangplank, slick when wet, led from the back of the house to the shower and outhouse. A shower in New Guinea involved a reservoir of rain water and a dipping pan for pouring the water over the body. A chicken coop and a *gudang,* or storage shed, completed the compound.

The Raschers immediately set about learning Indonesian. When President Sukarno later claimed Netherlands New Guinea for Indonesia, it was partly with the justification that since the people in Netherlands New Guinea spoke Indonesian, they belonged with Indonesia.

Indonesian is an extremely phonetic language and much simpler to learn than the tribal languages. Someone could be found who could understand and speak it in most tribes in New Guinea. TEAM missionaries generally settled into specific tribes and learned the tribal language, sometimes working many years to commit it to writing. The fact that Larry and Shirley learned to speak Indonesian well equipped them for later work from tribe to tribe.

MAF pilots performed important services for them, and became their good friends. They brought in their supplies, fresh vegetables and the mail. They provided transportation from one station to another. Flying conditions in New Guinea were hazardous in the best of weather, and they met the challenge.

Larry and Pilot Dave Hoisington developed their own routine. As Dave taxied the Cessna in on its floats, Larry called to him from the riverbank: "Hoisington! You got the meat and the mail?"

"No," Dave shouted.

"Then you get outta here!"

Dave goosed the engine, circled over the river and brought the plane back in.

"Hey Rascher, you got coffee and cookies for me?" Dave yelled on the second approach.

"Not for you!" Larry waved him on, and Dave circled again.

Doris and Phyllis, the young single TEAM missionaries, lived in the aluminum house next door. They

eagerly included the Raschers in their ritual of board
games or Rook card games on Friday nights. Shirley
loved to have company, so she invited the women over
for supper and game night at their house. The first
Friday night, Shirley was setting the table when Larry
whispered urgently from the front porch: "Shirley,
come here, quick! Look what's coming." The two women
were teetering across the marshy yard in high heels
and stockings. This was to be social life at the outpost
of Kokonao.

Unfortunately, in the eyes of the natives, Doris and
Phyllis became Larry's other wives. The Mimikas' important men had many wives. Surely this *tuan*, this white
man, couldn't be content with just one. The situation
was a severe nuisance and hindered the ability of the
four to work efficiently together. Larry could not ride in
a canoe with Doris and Phyllis or walk with them to a
toko without inciting gossip. If they were going to an
outlying village with him, the women had to take a
five-minute head start.

At home, Shirley worked alongside a succession of
house helpers. None stayed long for various reasons.
Actually, Shirley would have preferred doing the work
herself because she liked cooking and managing her
own home. But the work provided income for some
Mimikas, and in stifling heat the daily chores were too
tedious for one person, particularly one with three
small children. The salt water and humidity made
constant wiping and dusting necessary. Stamps stuck
without licking. Carbon paper, batteries—everything
rusted or mildewed. Floors and porches were swept
with *sapu lidi* brooms made from the spines of palm
leaves and mopped daily. Regiments of tiny ants regularly
assaulted the counter top.

Laundry water was heated in the kettle behind their
house and the worst of the dirt was scrubbed out on a
board before the clothes were dumped into the belt-

driven Maytag, which frequently broke down. Then the clothes were hung out on the line in the chance it wouldn't rain. Laundry was an almost daily ritual. Perspiration necessitated at least two changes of clothes a day.

Shirley became adept at cooking macaroni and wild boar, and the native staple sago and smak (Spam) fifty ways each. Fresh dairy products weren't available, so they used powdered milk and canned butter and cheese. She made the children eat their vegetables, which Keith learned to drop inconspicuously and work with his toe into a crack in the wood floor.

The Rascher household routine included breakfast, family devotions, morning chores, the big meal mid-day, a nap, a shower, and work resuming at about 4:00 p.m. Offices and *tokos* closed midday and reopened in the cooler late afternoon.

Home was the hub of all family activity. There was no competition from a TV or telephone. But there was plenty of company—even at the end of the world: pilots or missionaries passing through, visiting government dignitaries, executives from the American mining company up the coast, Sunday evening coffees for the Mimikas. If there was a meeting, it was in their living room. If anyone came to town, he stayed at the Raschers'.

But the Raschers had a problem in Kokonao. They discovered all too quickly that they were viewed as the "false religion."

They continued the Lovestrand's practice of holding Sunday evening coffees for Mimikas in their home. A few would come, sometimes coercing family members or friends to join them.

But a spy skulked behind a coconut palm: "Don't you want your sons and daughters to be able to attend our school?" a priest would inquire later, when the miscreants were summoned. "Do you not want them to participate in the parades?" The four village chiefs in Kokonao were Catholic and could be prevailed upon to apply pressure. Teachers in the Catholic grammar and high schools were paid according to the number of students in school, so they, too, would make defection uncomfortable.

Then there was tobacco, which was distributed by the priests, even to children, as a reward for attendance. Crocodile hunters used tobacco to advantage, too. For a few handfuls a native would sell a fresh water crocodile skin worth $200 or a brighter-skinned salt water croc worth $500.

Who would want to displease the Catholic church, which had brought civilization to the Mimikas—medical treatment, a school and a belief? And tobacco. Who would want to cross the priest who was as powerful in Kokonao as any government official? Who were these Americans anyway? Who, indeed, Larry and Shirley often wondered.

Only one Mimika family attended services at Humassey's church when the Raschers arrived. The other church attendants were Protestant government workers, mostly Biakers. Why this one Mimika, Mehel, was so proud to be a Protestant was a mystery to them. As time went on, however, their church tended to draw more disgruntled and discontent Mimikas.

Mehel was old and proud and whined that Larry didn't give him things. The Raschers bought their week's supply of sago from Mehel until they went along into the jungle one day to watch his wife prepare it. She took a handful of crude sago from the heart of a cut sago palm, spit into it, and squeezed it through a sieve. Thereafter they bought sago from Mehel sometimes but fed it to the chickens.

Squirming on the benches of the Protestant church, Larry and Shirley were well aware of another problem. Pastor Humassey, a slight, balding man, peered down at his parishioners from a tall pulpit in the tiny church. With all the volume and drama he could muster he drew out and accentuated every word—words devoid of spiritual meaning. It was a lifeless ritual.

Bapak Humassey was building a bulwark against Catholicism among the government workers. He felt that if Larry and Shirley wanted to build a bulwark of faith in Jesus Christ among the Mimika, they could patrol the native villages along the rivers to preach. The Sunday pulpit was Humassey's.

Week after week the sermons dragged on. Larry and Shirley longed for a chance to worship and celebrate God's Son and life, abundant life. And to be able to help free the Mimika from superstition and fear.

They enjoyed patrolling, which got them closer to the native people, even though it was not easy to communicate the Good News to a Mimika. So many concepts like salvation, atonement, and unconditional love were foreign to his thought, much less to his language. To bridge the gulf to understanding took a patient Christian willing to chew the fat, willing to relate with a native over a long period of time. Willing to learn his wants, his fears, his needs, his language and idioms, to earn his respect and trust. Larry and Shirley sought to do this on many visits to villages over stretches of time.

Three things came of their growing frustration in Kokonao. There was an inevitable split within Humassey's church. A small band stepped out with the Raschers. They were all believers who wanted to grow in the application of God's Word to their lives: two single male postal workers, the families of two male government nurses (one of them, Wakum, a hot-tempered man, wept openly as they sang "Power in the Blood"), a government-subsidized native teacher who had come to teach their TEAM school, Dr. Tjoa from the hospital, a handful of Mimika school children, the

Mimika Mehel's family, and Serguis Pai, a Biaker and a Bible school graduate who became the church's pastor. What the new church conspicuously lacked, to Larry and Shirley, was the presence of more Mimikas.

They turned more and more of their energies to reaching the Mimikas in smaller outlying villages, which they patrolled by dugout canoe, staying a few days to a few weeks each time. They found that the villages farther from Kokonao were more responsive to the gospel and less controlled by the Catholic establishment. From their work at the village of Amar there grew a church, school and air strip.

Third, their longing grew to work among an unreached tribe that knew nothing of the Catholic church—or of any church—or school, or the conventions of civilized man. They dreamed of a tribe that would realize its need of a Savior and would call forth all the Raschers could give. They did not want to abandon the work among the Mimika, but they hoped they could make contact with a tribe that knew it needed what they could give.

The sense of futility in Kokonao sapped their energy and took its toll on their health. MAF Pilot George Boggs was on a veggie run delivering fresh produce to the south coast mission stations. It appeared to him that Larry and Shirley had lost weight and were alarmingly tired. He loaded the family on the plane for a weekend at his home on the north coast at Nabire.

Larry and Shirley swam in the ocean and poked around on the beach with the children, alone except for a huddle of natives frying fish. Their bodies rested, their spirits revived. Their perspectives shifted.

The Psalms were particularly precious to Shirley. She found generous portions of truth in them for her. In Nabire the Lord used a psalm to give Shirley fresh vision and encouragement.

Surely God is good to Israel,
To those who are pure in heart!
But as for me, my feet came close to stumbling;
My steps had almost slipped.
For I was envious of the arrogant,
As I saw the prosperity of the wicked. . . .
My flesh and my heart may fail;
But God is the strength of my heart
and my portion forever.

Psalm 73:1–3, 26, NAS

"Shirley," He seemed to say, "Shirley, you have been preoccupied with the priests and what they get away with and how they hinder your work. I will be your strength. I'm all you need. The work is not yours or Larry's, it is Mine. I have called you, and My grace and strength are sufficient for you."

Larry's frustration eased, too, as he later prepared a sermon on the Beatitudes for their Kokonao church. Matthew 5:6 caught his heart:

Blessed are those who hunger and thirst for
righteousness, for they shall be satisfied. (NAS)

The word *satisfied,* he discovered, meant to be completely filled, almost to the point of choking. He intended to quest for more of the Lord and to leave the results of his labors to God.

PIRIMAPUN

Larry began his work as an itinerant builder on a TEAM hospital at the south coast government outpost of Pirimapun.

Pirimapun was wild. It marked the westernmost frontier of the Asmat tribe, most notorious of the cannibals. A handful of government officials lived there to patrol the Asmat and keep the peace, along with TEAM missionaries Dr. Ken and Sylvia Dresser. But by and large the natives of the area were naked and mud-caked and disinterested in civilization.

Nearly 400 natives lived in the village of Pirimapun; they inhabited nine large long-houses and several smaller ones all built on stilts. Each woman had her own cooking fire raised off the wood floor on a bed of clay. This kept her and her children warm, and her husband as he came and went (most men had more than one wife), and it was always ready for roasting sago or fish. The houses were without windows, and their interiors were sooty and dark. Beds were grass mats, and the skull of an ancestor who could give protection from evil spirits served as a pillow. Shields, bows and arrows, and spears stood ready in the long houses. Many of the men wore bamboo through their noses and shaved the front of their scalps with bamboo.

None of them knew then that the ocean several miles

away at Cook's Bay would in a few years devour the swamps clear up to Pirimapun and beyond, including the TEAM hospital. For now the ocean was coyly out of sight to the south. Native children at Pirimapun cooled themselves playing in the knee-deep mud at low tide among the pelicans and crocodiles, which lumbered away at the commotion.

Plans for the hospital at Pirimapun included a porch for waiting, a treatment room, an operating room, a laboratory, a ward, and a storeroom. However, the native patients would have nothing to do with beds and plates and silverware. Instead they stayed in a long house reserved for them out back. The hospital ward would serve the missionary or government worker about to deliver a baby or needing treatment. A guest house was to be built for the missionary patient's family.

Larry had been learning about building with native materials by watching the natives and Dutch carpenters and by talking to fellow missionaries. The 4 x 4's used for the frame were fitted together on the ground with the peg on the end of one plank fitting exactly into the hole in the adjoining one. One or two carpenters were able to build the frame, labeling the boards which fit together as they worked. The actual raising of the structure on its piers was an event, *ramai ramai,* in which the whole village became involved, like a barn raising. Planks, siding, or *gaba gaba* was put up for walls. The roofs were thatch or palm leaves or sheets of corrugated metal.

At the prospect of using Asmat natives to do the building at Pirimapun, Larry brought Evert with him as a foreman. Evert was a quiet, young, native carpenter from Kokonao whom Larry knew to be a believer in Christ and whom Larry had entrusted with his own household carpentry work.

Beautiful dark-brown ironwood was cut and prepared at the TEAM sawmill in Ayam and brought to

Pirimapun by boat. The ironwood was so hard that a hole had to be drilled for each nail, and each nail lubricated with drain oil. Progress was very slow—the natives had no sense of time or hurry. If morning dawned dark and rainy, no one stirred from the long houses until the day brightened. But Larry had a knack for getting native workers to show up and stay at the task. He loved to tease them to put them at ease. He joined them in a good laugh at himself when the *tuan* made a mistake. He admired the skill with which the natives worked with the materials they had at hand.

Larry was proud of the hospital building when it was completed. It had louvered windows with screens, double glass doors, an aluminum roof, and stood on cement rather than ironwood pilings. The ground was so soft that Larry had found if they twisted ironwood pilings into the ground they would keep going down and eventually vanish. It was more American-looking than buildings Larry later built as he became more familiar with using trusses, for example, and fewer rafters like the natives did.

Larry was also proud of Evert and offered him one of the apples brought to the station by an MAF plane on a veggie run—six apples per missionary family. Larry watched in dismay as Evert grimaced and nearly threw up the fruit that was so foreign to his taste.

At first the Rascher children disliked the pinching, touching and staring of their smelly, naked neighbors who ate bananas skins and all. Asmaters had seen white government workers, missionaries, and priests, but *tuan* children were strange and interesting. As their presence became more commonplace, the Rascher kids found playmates and enjoyed rides on the shoulders of the native men. The natives loved to hold the *tuan* children and carry them around.

Shirley settled the family into the "Decca House," a

prefab house which had been built by the Decca Company when they installed a radio communication system at Pirimapun. It was vacated when the company finished and quickly left. The Raschers used the furnishings left there and kept their own household goods at Kokonao. They were all grasping Indonesian quickly and could at least communicate with some Asmaters in Indonesian.

It was a challenge, Shirley found, to train Asmaters as house helpers. Their house boy had crossed eyes, the expanse of white eyeballs startling against his dark skin. Each morning when he arrived for work Shirley handed him a bar of soap and a bucket of water for washing himself. He would then put on the pants and shirt that hung on the back of the door. He left the clothes at the house; otherwise they'd be filthy the next day.

Procedures as simple as washing the dishes took lots of training and reinforcement. The boy didn't see the need for dishes, much less the need to keep washing them. Larry walked into the kitchen one day to find him licking the plates before putting them in the water, his crossed eyes beaming over the rim of a plate.

News traveled through the waterways, perhaps by crocodile hunters, that a *tuan* family, the Raschers, were staying at Pirimapun. The *tuan* was building an ironwood house, it was told. He paid for labor with machetes, pants, fish hooks, cups, cooking pots, knives, and axes.

One village thought of a way they might capitalize upon having *tuans* in the neighborhood. At midday the Raschers heard chanting—a sea of voices in front of their house. They looked out from the six-foot-high Decca house on the people of Oscanep, a village three rivers over. As far as they could see were naked black bodies under hats woven from river grasses. "Hats, hats, you want to buy hats?" they chanted. The wide-brimmed, straw-like hats were stiff, had no give, and were worthless as head coverings. Besides, if an Oscanep man had worn it, it likely bore fleas and lice. The Raschers greeted the Oscaneps, but did not buy hats.

Larry befriended a heavy, white-haired old chief of the village at Pirimapun. Bolder toward the *tuans* than most Asmaters, he began to come to the Decca house and sit on the porch, where he invariably fell asleep; and the family had to walk over his sprawling, naked body to come and go from the house. But the man meant no harm, so they left him alone. Uninvited natives in the house were another matter—they were not allowed.

One native lived with them for a while: Sammy, an infant twin, whom the Rascher children called "Shine Eyes" because his eyes shone in the dark. It was the practice of native parents to kill the weaker twin at birth, figuring that the mother couldn't feed both and one would die eventually anyway. The Dressers had intervened for Sammy, but Sylvia Dresser was too ill at the time to care for him. Shirley had the heart for more children, so she willingly took on the job. Sammy had chronic diarrhea and was pitifully thin and listless, except for those big, shining eyes. Perhaps Sammy was allergic to milk, but there was no one to nurse him. Shirley fed him bottled milk from the clinic. Whenever Sammy grew somewhat stronger, his parents came for him and took him home into the jungle. A few weeks later they brought him back thin and panting for breath.

The time came when the parents didn't return with him. The death of a child was commonplace to natives in Netherlands New Guinea, but it came hard to the Raschers.

Five-year-old Kathy wanted a baby badly to carry around like her native friends did. She knew that her mommy was pregnant and getting bigger while they lived in Pirimapun, but one day Shirley wasn't big anymore. Kathy didn't know what had happened, but she shared her mother's sadness.

The Rascher family took their fun where they could find or create it. On Sundays, after worship, the midday meal and a rest, they enjoyed a Sunday treat. It could be a boat ride, a picnic and swimming at the ocean, or maybe board games and popcorn balls on rainy afternoons.

There were other days too when the treats just happened. Often it was because they saw the possibilities of humor in the naîveté of the natives.

One day, when building was at a standstill awaiting supplies, Larry grew restless. A pair of old, wide-plank water skis had been left in the Decca house, and Larry took the occasion to try them. Dr. Dresser had a sixteen-foot fiberglass outboard with a forty-horsepower motor that he used for patrolling outlying villages.

Larry fetched the skis and his three little helpers. He pulled Doc Dresser from the clinic, leaving a government-employed nurse in charge. Larry seated Keith, Kathy and Chipper in the front of the boat to help weigh it down and attached a rope to the stern.

At the whine of a motor on the river, the entire village ran to the banks. But when the doctor roared by with *Tuan* Rascher walking on the water, they fled to the jungle. The Rascher children squealed with glee.

Larry and Shirley took time in Pirimapun to observe as the Dressers treated diseases common to the swamps: malaria, dysentery, pneumonia, oozing tropical ulcers, and filaria, which untreated develops into elephantiasis. The Dressers routinely dressed spear and arrow wounds and extracted teeth.

It was reassuring to live close to a doctor in the swamps of New Guinea. One day Chip swallowed a fish bone in an attempt to prove himself as invincible as the natives. Larry ran down the path and along the airstrip to the Dressers' clinic with Chip slung over his shoulder. The doctor used forceps to dislodge the bone and remove it.

Of course "Doc Dressers" were rare in the swamps, so he was frequently off treating patients in other villages. At one such time Keith sustained his first of several broken arms. The Dutch government had built a cement bridge over a creek at Pirimapun. Its presence and construction were completely incongruent with its surroundings. Keith was fascinated, and he hopped right up. He imagined he was a native of the highlands, crossing a rushing stream on a fallen tree. But when he fell, the ditch was more hard than wet.

Out of nowhere The Beaver, a huge Dutch amphibious plane, landed at Pirimapun within minutes of the fall. At Larry's request it transported Keith and Larry to the hospital at Agats (the southern, main government post of the Asmat), where the arm was set.

Both Keith and Chip loved the sort of talk-to-the-pilot, right-over-the-jungle flying that had become commonplace for them. MAF pilots were their heroes. Chip claimed that the second time Keith broke his arm he scrambled up from the ground and said, "My arm's broken! Call the plane!"

At last the day arrived for the dedication of the hospital building at Pirimapun. It was attended by Dr. Vernon Mortenson, the general director of TEAM, who was then visiting the field in West Irian. The completion of the building was a great excuse for a people who love celebrations. The *tuan* missionaries and government representatives made speeches. The local natives danced in rows, like waves—back and forth, back and forth—to the beating of drums through the day and the night.

The wait for lumber to complete the outer walls of the medical guest house had no foreseeable end, so the Raschers were sent to Manokwari for the summer of 1963 to complete a new dining hall for the Bible school at Saowi. Evert the carpenter went with them to help. After completion of the dining hall, Evert attended the Bible school at Saowi and went on to work as a teacher, evangelist, and pastor to tribal people. At summer's end the Raschers returned to Kokonao, just ahead of an epidemic in the Asmat.

CHOLERA

Four-year-old Chip Rascher took a minute to scratch the rash of sand fly bites on his leg as he climbed into his tiny dugout canoe. The tide was coming in, and he'd waited for it all morning. He was in his own backyard in Kokonao, and he knew Mom would only let him go as far as the bridge one way and the path in front of the house the other way. As Chip stood in his boat, paddling on one side and then the other, he imagined himself following his dad up the river, deep into the swamps.

Larry had traded for a Mimika dugout canoe, which had been adzed with an axe and burned on the bottom to seal the wood and purge it of ship worms. Larry sawed off the back tip of the canoe, fitted a wood transom into the hole, and mounted a Johnson outboard motor on it. Chip's canoe was made from the cut-off tip. Chip nailed in some wood to form his transom. It leaked, but he packed mud into the seams, and when the mud dried it was seaworthy.

Larry continually had to service his two outboard motors and the Briggs & Stratton engines that powered his tools, and Chip was his chief helper. Chip's job was to clean the greasy parts with gasoline so they were slick and clean. Later, when Keith and Chip got a little older, Larry would give them a dugout canoe with a three-and-a-half horsepower outboard motor. Chip would help keep the motor humming and take the boat upriver for long periods. Keith would be less interested in fixing the motor than in spearfishing from the boat when the motor was ready.

On this morning Larry had left in an eighteen-foot fiberglass outboard with three male government nurses from the hospital at Kokonao, Doris Florin, and Marge Smith. Marge was a young single woman who had come to Kokonao with TEAM Irian when Phyllis Griffiths got married and left. The boat was loaded with medical supplies and a pot and stove for boiling needles. Cholera had broken out in the neighboring Asmat tribe. An Indonesian government official at Kokonao had asked this team to patrol all the Mimika villages, inoculating the natives before the disease spread.

The rule of Netherlands New Guinea had recently been transferred by the United Nations to the 13,000-island Republic of Indonesia. The province was now called West Irian.

Indonesia gained the oil and mineral wealth of West Irian and a sparsely populated land mass to which it could move transmigrants from the teeming island of Java.

Of concern at the moment was cholera on the south coast. Stories had come out of the Asmat tribe of seventy in a village dying within a few days—seventeen in one night at Pirimipun. Cholera bacteria is spread in food and water contaminated by those with the disease. Flies do their part in transmittal. The bacteria settles in the intestines and produces severe inflammation that leads to general body poisoning. With diarrhea and vomiting, the loss of body fluid becomes so intense that within three days the changes in body chemistry can bring on shock and death.

Fear preceded the scourge running through the

swamps. Native villages did what they knew to ward off the evil spirits bringing this awful death. At Saman, up river from Pirimapun in Asmat territory, four or five young boys were placed on a platform. Through the night the natives threw burning sticks at them, burning them severely, to appease the malevolent spirits.

The Catholic priest at Kokonao was sure that cholera had been brought into the Asmat on the floats of an MAF plane. The first known cases had been diagnosed close to where the plane had recently landed.

The Asmat burial practice of leaving the dead to rot on a grass mat atop a burial rack—where the body became prey to birds and the village dogs—did not help contain the spread of the disease. The government had sent policemen to torch the many burial racks at Pirimapun, angering the natives.

As Larry and the team worked their way through the maze of rivers, they followed a strict procedure. When they approached a village, they would kill the motor some distance from shore and call to the villagers. "Is anyone sick among you? Has anyone died in the last few days?" If the village answered them in the negative, which they had all done, the team went ashore, set water to boiling on a kerosene burner to sterilize needles, and lined up all the people.

Larry's job was to continue boiling needles, which had to be used over and over—100 times if they lasted—and to sharpen them with a whetstone when they got too dull. Larry squatted over his stove, thankful for his lot. The natives' skin was taut, toughened by exposure and a foul-smelling ringworm that built up along the skin. The nurses were bending lots of needles on leathery arms.

An adult Mimika could take the shot without flinching. But once a child in line began to cry, all the children wailed.

As they finished up at the oceanside village of

Muwadi—a week into the job and midway through their assigned eastern half of Mimika territory—Larry left his pot long enough to ask the chief if they had inoculated everyone. "No, *Tuan*," he replied. "Half of our people are away in the jungle gathering sago for us."

"Well then, we'll go on to the other villages," Larry said. In five days we'll be back here on our way home. I want you to have all the rest waiting here for us. You understand, Chief, that this is very important. In five days we'll be here. Don't let anyone go back to the jungle."

"Yes, *Tuan*."

Five days later the natives of Muwadi were there, lining the beach, animated and gesturing frantically to them to come. They closed quickly around the outboard. "*Tuan*, it is among us. Two have died and three lie sick now." The food gatherers had returned with sago and cholera.

The team conferred and agreed that they should stay and inoculate those they had missed; Larry would go back to Kokonao to get the doctor and a second team of nurses who could begin treatment and intravenous feedings. It was nearly 5:00 p.m. Larry had on his uniform: a T-shirt, shorts and flip-flops. He hadn't eaten since breakfast. The jungle would be dark at 6:00, but he couldn't wait until morning. Fortunately there would be moonlight that night.

The tide would be out for several hours. Larry pointed the boat up the coast, his motor at medium speed. The boat slapped along on choppy little waves fueled by afternoon winds on the ocean. He was making decent time and hoped to be in Kokonao in about two hours.

For twenty or thirty miles he bounced along the coast, as a fiery sun slipped through coral lining and into the blue night-pocket of the sea. His adrenalin was pumping, masking his hunger. It was a relief to be able to act, to do something, to help in an emergency. He prayed for the panic-stricken people of Muwadi.

Then, as he neared the Kekwa river mouth, one hard slap of a wave slit a crack in the fiberglass along the seam where the side of the boat and its bottom joined. Since it was mid-boat on the left side, and the steering wheel was in the middle of the boat on the right, Larry was barely able to peer over the steering wheel and stretch out his left leg so that his rubber flip-flop covered the crack. In the breakers at the river mouth the motor stalled and the gears quit working properly. Larry leapt to the back of the boat, started the motor, put it in gear, and throttled it up to speed. He then sprang back to the steering wheel and his left foot's critical position.

Larry worked his way up the Kekwa to a little tributary which would take him across and into Kokonao. Near the mouth of the Kekwa, two Mimika policemen heard his boat and called him over. *"Mari sini!"* Larry lurched back to turn off the motor, replaced his left foot and steered toward them.

"What's the trouble?"

The government was cutting off all traffic up and down the rivers to prevent the spread of cholera. "If people in the villages need food we will bring it to them, but no one may pass into this river," one said. "There are guards at the other end as well."

Larry explained his situation. "I must get to Kokonao tonight to get the doctor and nurses." Larry eyed the two men. "And I need one of you to go with me."

They talked among themselves. One evidently thought more of the ride to Kokonao with Larry than spending the night in their lean-to with the mosquitoes. He climbed into the boat bringing a two-cell flashlight, a poncho, and the dinner he'd been eating—a smoked fish on a porcelain plate. "You watch with the flashlight,"

Larry instructed. "Shine it to the left and I'll steer left. When you see a log or mud, or whatever, you yell and I'll steer to the right. Then you come around behind me and shine the light to the right. As they zigzagged up the river, it began to rain without warning, a straight-down pounding rain. There was no more moonlight.

At a bend in the river the boat suddenly raised up out of the water, then slammed down before Larry could cut the motor. The men looked at each other. There was no sound but the rain. "We made it. I think we'll be all right," Larry said, and started the motor. But soon they were standing in water to their ankles. They steered the boat to the soggy riverbank.

Larry untied the motor from the back of the boat. Lifting it onto his shoulder, he staggered forward, mud sucking at his legs up to the knees. His eye was on the fork of a tree about eight feet up, a half-block trudge away. He lifted the motor to the fork of the tree and wedged it in securely.

The boat was submerged to the gunwales and there was no way to pull it in, so both men began to bail—Larry with a paddle and the policeman with his plate. As they bailed they inched the boat to higher ground.

By midnight they had worked the boat well back from the river, but the tide was coming in. They could see the hole, a gash a foot long and three inches wide, at the stern of the boat. The flap of fiberglass was still attached and slid open and closed. They turned the boat around and slid the gash into the mud to close it while they bailed the bow. "*Tuan*, I will shoot the gun and get help," the policeman suggested a bit too eagerly. He shot off two volleys, but only the birds-of-paradise, the parrots, and the egrets seemed to hear through the rain.

Then they rested, sitting with their backs against the stern of the boat and their feet toward the lower bow, huddled under the policeman's government-issue poncho. When the rain stopped, they used the poncho for protection from the feasting mosquitoes. Through the night whenever the water in the boat rose to their feet, the men bailed some more. They tied the line from the bow of the boat over one tree branch and the line from the stern over another. As the tide lifted the boat they kept adjusting the ropes to keep the boat on top of the water.

Dawn and high tide found the men perched in the tree, the outboard motor now barely a foot out of water. Regiments of tiny sand flies had succeeded the mosquitoes, biting more viciously. Each man slapped himself with a limb until the leaves all fell off, then tore off another limb.

Larry took stock of their situation. A nasty cut in his left foot stung from the salt water. The blood from his foot, and his partner's smoked fish—which had drifted away when the boat swamped—were both come-ons to crocodiles. Any thought of swimming the rivers to Kokonao vanished.

They were hungry and terribly thirsty. With one of them facing one direction on the river and one the opposite, they both yelled for help, in Indonesian and in Mimika, but there was no answer. They were well aware that all river traffic had ceased. Shirley would not yet be expecting Larry. The day steamed up. Turbid water below and the exertion of the night made them drowsy. Larry prayed in earnest. He confessed all the sins he could think of, going back weeks, months, years. "Lord," he said, "You've got to work a miracle and save us. I know that if David Brainerd or Praying Hyde or some of those saints were here, they would trust you for a miracle, and you would do it. I don't have that kind of faith, but I want to believe you'll do something. Shirley doesn't know where I am and Lord, please, you've got to get us out of here."

They began calling out again. Tired as he was, Larry

could still boom out with his preaching voice. Nothing. At last they heard a faint drone growing distinctly closer and louder. The policeman remembered that government boats were going to deliver food to villages. They called out and Larry prayed, but the noise diminished, then vanished. The boat had taken advantage of the morning calm and traveled by ocean. Larry prayed it would return by river, but it didn't.

Discouragement colored Larry's monologue. "If you're not going to answer this prayer, the problem must be with Larry Rascher. Am I not yielded enough to you, Lord? Don't I trust you enough? I don't have what it takes to be a missionary. I know you answered our prayers and you brought us out here, but if I get back to Kokonao I'm going to write our supporting churches and tell them I just don't have what it takes and we'll go home and I'll work for my dad." A stupor was setting in and both men would doze, then resume calling.

Larry awoke with a start as he began to slide from his perch. The shock sharpened his senses. As he resumed his prayer and introspection he was thinking more clearly. "I'm sorry, Lord. That's just what Satan would want, isn't it—for me to up and quit. Lord, even if you don't answer my prayer, I still believe you made heaven and earth. And I still believe you sent your Son to save me, and my buddy here, and the Mimika. As long as I live, I'll serve you. No matter whether I die today or next month or in thirty years, I'll serve you every day I live." He called again, louder this time, more hopefully. Nothing happened, but his spirit was at peace. He resumed with vigor his battle with the annoying flies.

This time they heard a diesel motor, hearty and unmistakable on the river. A government launch was headed from the distant post of Akimuga to the hospital at Kokonao with a native woman who was hemorrhaging from delivering a child. The motor was loud enough that the launch passed them by without hearing their cries. But a passenger happened to catch sight of them in the trees, and the boat circled back.

"We had not planned to use the river," the government official said to Larry as they headed toward Kokonao, towing the outboard. "Yesterday when the ocean got rough we stopped at the village of Kekwa. The ocean was calm this morning, but for no real reason we decided to take the river route instead." Larry breathed a silent prayer of gratitude.

Late that morning the Rascher kids saw Daddy limping up the path to their house and they called to Shirley. His T-shirt was ripped, he was dirtier than they'd ever seen him, and he had a stubble of beard. Their tin can house had never looked so good to Larry, nor had his wife or his children. Shirley cooked him a big breakfast while he showered. He slept for a while, then mounted his outboard motor on a cut-off dugout canoe he borrowed at the *toko* and set out for Muwadi with a fresh medical team.

Not until sometime afterward would Larry hear that the whole expedition may have been in vain. There was some question as to whether the serum used was for the right strain of cholera. Anyone they had inoculated could perhaps have caught it—Larry included.

But then who's to say what effort is in vain? They had helped do what they could for the people. And Larry had truly surrendered all his life to God.

KOKONAO

In Kokonao there was no such thing as a time conflict. No one would have to miss the community Christmas service for boy scouts or bowling league. Everyone would be there—government workers, priests, and Mimikas—and Larry was to preach.

A new community building had been erected in Kokonao soon after the Indonesian takeover. It was a rambling, crude structure of frame and *gaba gaba* with a dirt floor and low walls. The upper half of the walls was open for moving air. For the grand occasion of the Christmas service it had a borrowed, government-owned public address system; the people loved P.A.'s.

Christmas in Kokonao involved a week of festivities—mostly visiting around to friends and relatives—and a Christmas service to which the entire community was invited. The religious figures in the community passed around the job of preaching the Christmas service. The priest and *Bapak* Humassey had both preached since the Raschers arrived; it was Larry's turn.

Larry prayed over and worked on this message for weeks. It must be delivered in Indonesian and written out ahead of time for the priest, *Bapak* Humassey, and the post officials to approve.

The center was festive inside and out, with garlands

made of palm leaf fronds. The Christmas tree up front was a banana tree stalk stuffed with feathery cassorina tree branches. The boughs held lighted candles in bamboo holders and ornaments woven from coconut palm leaves.

Government workers and priests sat on the front benches on that muggy December night. Hundreds of Mimikas stood around the walls on the inside and the outside.

Korwa, an Indonesian male government nurse and a Christian, led a choir in old Dutch Christmas songs and *O Come All Ye Faithful* in Indonesian.

Then Larry's turn came. The P.A. was turned down, then off, as Larry warmed to his subject. He proclaimed the wonder of the Savior's birth and death to whomever would receive it.

> *[Jesus], although He existed in the form of God, did not regard equality with God a thing to be grasped, but emptied Himself, taking the form of a bondservant, and being made in the likeness of men. And being found in appearance as a man, He humbled Himself by becoming obedient to the point of death, even death on a cross. Therefore also God highly exalted Him, and bestowed on Him the name which is above every name, that at the name of Jesus every knee should bow, of those who are in heaven, and on earth, and under the earth, and that every tongue should confess that Jesus Christ is Lord, to the glory of God the Father.*
>
> *Phil. 2:6–11, NAS*

He paced the front of the room, gesturing and talking with such volume and animation that his face grew red till he finally stopped and took a breath. Jesus Christ wasn't born in Bethlehem to teach or to work miracles. He was God, born as a man later to die on a cross so that all men could be free from bondage to evil spirits and to sin.

This was not the predictable read sermon of the priest or of *Bapak* Humassey. The audience was spellbound in the soft tropical night, so far away from Judea or *I'm Dreaming of a White Christmas*. This was a new message. The *tuan* seemed so sure of what he said.

In coming weeks there would be no particular change in the attendance at church or their Sunday evening coffees, although years later a Mimika saw Larry in the capital city of Jayapura and said he remembered Larry's Christmas sermon. Harassment from the Catholic hierarchy would continue unabated. But on this night Larry gave the gospel with all the joy of his calling.

Six-year-old Kathy was so proud of her father who preached so well and meant what he said. She was proud of the hush in the room that showed the respect of all these people who listened. Kathy caught the eyes of her friends Iche, Ludi and Mia to see if they were proud, too. The four of them had recited Scripture verses together as part of the program.

On Christmas Eve, Chip tailed Larry out the front door, down the steps, and to the back of the house where Larry let Chip plug in the generator. Father and son stood in the yard admiring their Christmas tree through the window. Their aluminum tree was ablaze with colored lights. The tree had straight limbs—amazing in a climate where everything drooped. Its needles looked like little strips of aluminum foil. Among the lights were paper chains and Styrofoam ornaments that Keith and Kathy and Chip had made.

The tree had been a triumph of their undauntable Grandma and Grandpa Rascher. They had searched for an aluminum Christmas tree in June in St. Louis until they located one in storage at a Ben Franklin store. They shipped the tree in three separate boxes. This meant that for months the family had two-thirds of a tree and speculated as to whether the center section would arrive for Christmas, which it did.

The tree provided the only light in their home, and at that hour the only light in Kokonao, an oasis in the swamp. Larry read the Christmas story from the Bible. They sat quietly with their thoughts and the pretty lights, munching on crispy, sweet Hoosier cakes, Larry's favorite, since Christmas Eve was Larry's birthday.

There was no sense even bothering about Santa Claus. The children knew that anything new they received came from the barrels in the *gudang.* There was joy in just being at home together. They were thankful that that year Larry had been able to tell the village about Christmas.

The next morning Chip and Keith dominated the living room with a new race car set. Kathy arranged life for a new doll. Paint-by-number sets and other gifts were strewn about.

Marge and Margaret came from next door for Christmas dinner. Margaret Stringer had replaced Doris Florin, who married and left Kokonao. Marge was straightforward and was satisfied with her school to teach, her garden, and several pets. She loved animals and did not allow Keith and Chip to hunt birds around her coconut trees. When Marge was cleaning out her *gudang* and a rat jumped down her blouse, she exclaimed "Oh!"—took it out calmly—and kept cleaning. Cooking was a nuisance to Marge. Whatever was on hand she'd usually throw in one pot.

Margaret, a linguist, was sensitive and prone to emotional highs and lows. If a native language helper didn't show up, Margaret would struggle with hurt feelings. But oh, could Margaret tell stories! Full moons were spectacular in Kokonao, without any street lights. Keith asked Margaret to take him on moonlight walks so he could listen to her stories in the magical night.

Both women became dedicated career missionaries in West Irian. They were good neighbors in Kokonao.

Another Christmas dinner guest was a God-send for Shirley. Dr. Tjoa Hin Hoat, an intelligent, single Chinese doctor, found himself assigned by the government to the hospital in Kokonao. Dr. Tjoa was a believer in Jesus Christ and attended the little TEAM church. Life on the post was lonely for him, and he sought the Raschers for fellowship and the comic relief of family life. At the time of their meeting, Shirley had amoebic dysentary and was becoming severely anemic. Dr. Tjoa made it his special project to nurse Shirley through the last month until their furlough year in the U.S. would begin in the summer of 1965.

Dr. Tjoa gave Shirley daily iron injections and strict instructions. She was to quit teaching first grade to the twins at home. (Larry took over, to Keith's delight.) She was to quit cooking. Once a day a large meal was prepared and brought in by two Indonesian ladies. Dr. Tjoa was an accomplished cook and would often come for dinner and prepare it himself. Shirley was not able to manage her household as she wanted. She had energy to do very little of anything, which was a great frustration. But she did receive good care and invaluable lessons in cooking with local ingredients.

The two Indonesian ladies delivered the meals in a handy aluminum cylinder-like container with four compartments stacked one on top of the other. Fried rice was in the bottom compartment. Next was soup with a coconut milk base and sere seasoning (citronella grass), flavored with a bit of fish or turtle. In the vegetable compartment was spinach or a squash or mashed sweet potatoes with fried pork filling. Inevitably, the vegetable was mixed with coconut milk and seasoned with *terasi*, a small crushed shrimp mixed with onion, garlic, and red pepper.

Terasi emitted a distinctive odor, the omen of a good cook in the Indonesian home. When Shirley took some to St. Louis on furlough Larry's dad said to Shirley,

"*You* may stay. But *that's* gotta go!" This became a family joke along with Larry's dad's standard comment each time one of them spoke Indonesian in front of him: "If you do, you'd better clean it up!"

The top compartment held fried meat, usually pork, or shrimp chips, koladi chips (similar to potato chips), or fried bananas. In addition, lemons, bananas, and coconuts grew on the island.

Shirley had always been a good cook. Now she became a good Indonesian cook, to the delight of her family and their many guests over the years.

The usual spectrum of kids lived in Kokonao. Keith, Kathy and Chip had his or her own circle of friends, not based on age but according to what they most liked to play. No particular group was "in" or "out."

Chip loved water and boats: dugout canoes and motor boats, diving and swimming.

Keith built huts in the jungle with friends, and hunted and fished.

Kathy played hopscotch, jump rope with vines, and marbles with Ludi, Iche, and Mia. They played in the big climbing tree in the front yard which had a swing.

Each little girl saved rubber bands. When they had enough, they attached them one to another to form a Chinese jump rope: a large, stretchy, rectangular cat's cradle held by two players like a double-dutch jump rope. The first player stepped inside the rectangle and hopped rhythmically in a pattern of her own creation. One foot and then the other went over a band and under it, wound around it and back out. Succeeding players had to copy her pattern exactly and not get tangled in the rubber bands. After each girl jumped one time, the bands were held higher and a new pattern was begun.

Each of Kathy's friends played through the days with an infant brother or sister tied to her back in a long piece of cloth. Kathy wished for a little brother or sister to tie onto hers. The girls played house by the hour, mimicking their mothers.

Marbles were big with the boys in Kokonao. Marble games were played on the dirt and sand paths, games of great precision. The marbles were flipped out from between the palms of both hands with a spin to them. Every boy carried around a sack of marbles. None had so many marbles that winning wasn't very important.

Marbles could be bought at the *tokos*. Larry brought tons of them from the States and paid for chores with them. Keith later won bags of marbles at boarding school; then while on vacation he lost them in a few weeks on the paths in Kokonao.

No one enjoyed life in West Irian more than Keith Rascher. Keith's white-blond hair was in a crew cut and his fair skin was always lobster red. He wore shorts with rocks or marbles bulging his pockets, a short-sleeved cotton shirt and no shoes. Often one arm was in a sling and he wore half a plastic soccer ball on his head. In the States kids only read in books about the sort of adventures Keith had. And Keith had the perfect guide.

Moses Kujera was the second of four sons of a policeman in Kokonao. They were natives of the Kaimana tribe, an interior tribe which had known civilization before the Mimika. Moses' father dealt in witchcraft. He was not a man to be crossed.

Moses was well into his teens but in the fifth grade in Kokonao's Protestant elementary school which Larry had built. This was not unusual in a culture where children may start school late—if at all—and may repeat grades a few times along the way. Moses had become a believer in Jesus Christ during his years in school.

He was tall, black and lanky, growing broad and powerful through the shoulders. He was quiet in school and around adults. But he had a particular natural savvy, a practical know-how that Larry appreciated immediately. Moses became Larry's right-hand man. When Larry sent Moses into the jungle to gather rattan vines for tying things or for a certain palm leaf for roofing, he knew Moses would be back quickly with the right thing. Larry couldn't find a job that Moses couldn't do easily, and Moses finished what he started. He could lift Larry's sixty-horsepower outboard motor onto his shoulder and carry it up the muddy river bank and along the path to the house. Chip would follow after with his three-and-a-half horse motor "like Moses."

What Moses did best for Larry Rascher was teach his eldest son to hunt and fish with skill. Moses was an uncanny outdoorsman. By age seven Keith was out hunting with a slingshot or bow and arrows, or spearfishing with Moses before the rest of the family awoke in the morning. Keith knew how far he was allowed to go and when he needed to be back, and he didn't abuse the rules. He was back with trophies, usually a number of small birds, before breakfast.

Sometimes while hunting the two stopped at a native garden and helped themselves to koladi. They built a fire, cooked, and ate it. Sticks around a garden, with strips of cloth and bottles, held black magic to keep robbers away. But for hunters the rules didn't apply.

Moses seemed to have inherited some of his father's magic and had *notions.* If his knee twitched, he had to go home. He knew somehow when it was time to go check their traps.

One day Keith, Moses and three teenage boys were fishing near the Mimika River mouth. They had strung trot lines between two poles a yard above the river, with several baited, dangling hooks. When the tide was in, the river rose and fish took the bait. When the tide went out the boys checked their lines and took off the fish. Usually they caught plenty of catfish. This day, for some reason, only gray puffer fish, with ballooned white bellies, hung from each line.

Keith was disappointed because puffer fish were poisonous. His folks told him never to eat them. Moses and the other boys knew they were, of course. But they also thought they knew what part of the fish was edible.

They began to build a fire on the beach to cook the fish. Keith couldn't believe they were really going to eat them, but they were, no matter what he said. Keith began walking home. He was afraid for his friends. No way was Keith going to eat a puffer fish.

Keith had tried to share Jesus Christ with his friends. He had given several of the boys Indonesian Bibles. He was not quite sure, though, that the boys would really take seriously what he said, because of things Keith had done with them. He had taken cans of corned beef for them out of the Rascher *gudang* (wasn't he a Rascher too?) to cook down at the river like they now cooked the puffer fish. But he had also taken eggplants with them from a man's large garden. Keith hoped the Lord would make up for where he had let Him down.

Keith didn't hear until morning how the boys had run to Kokonao. One fell dead in front of the hospital. The others had their stomachs pumped, including Moses, and were all right.

In the States the puffer fish episode might have been cigarettes behind a backyard fence. But where Keith learned about life, in West Irian, the stakes were higher. He learned that human heroes sometimes make mistakes and would sometimes let him down. He learned that obedience can be the difference between life and death. Big lessons for a little boy.

Diseases in Irian also pulled life and death closer together. Keith had been playing with Minggus (Moses' youngest brother) one night until dusk, when snakes and mosquitoes come out and children are called home. Early the next morning Keith ran to Minggus' house to continue the fun. He was told that Minggus couldn't play because he had contracted malaria during the night and was very ill.

Malaria was a fact of life in the swamps. Mosquitoes bore it everywhere. The Rascher family all took a malaria prophylactic in a glob of peanut butter on Sunday nights, but eventually they all got it anyway, Keith and Larry most often. The natives seemed more resistant to the disease, but when they had it, it was severe. Malaria is burning fever, then chills, then fever again. If the fever climbs too high the victim becomes delirious. Cerebral malaria can cause brain damage. Malaria can cause death, and it is a recurring disease. Effective treatment hinges on administering the right dosage of quinine soon enough. Minggus was given too much quinine, and when he recovered he was deaf. He was then called *Tulih,* deaf. What happened to Minggus didn't seem fair to Keith. Life held mysteries he did not like, but learned to accept.

Kathy Rascher's dream came true one August night in 1967 at the hospital Larry had built in Pirimapun. Gregory Rascher was born and was no sooner back home in Kokonao than sister Kathy began carrying him tied on her back. He napped there, a heavy, hot little ball against her back. She could feel his breathing. This was sheer joy—almost to the brim. With all these brothers Kathy still wanted a baby sister. That would be enough!

BOARDING SCHOOL

August 17th was Indonesian Independence Day, which complicated the matter of leaving for boarding school. Shirley had spent days packing the children's clothes—enough to last until Christmas vacation, but not more than the weight limit for the MAF float plane full of kids and their gear. Shirley welcomed the bustle because it delayed the coming void.

Keith and Kathy and Chip agreed with their parents' belief that it was best for them to get a good education and that the school at Sentani was the best place around to do so. When the time came, they were always excited to go back to their friends and their school. The boys more so than Kathy. But even Kathy knew that once the plane landed at Sentani she would be all right.

"Now you be brave, Mom," Kathy said to Shirley solemnly before they went to the river to wait for the plane.

"You, too," Shirley said, smiling and patting Kathy's hand.

"I just wish we didn't have to leave with everybody watching," Kathy laughed.

Independence Day meant that natives from all the villages along the rivers near Kokonao were at the government post for the celebrations. The landing of a float plane to pick up the *tuan* children was part of the show.

If Mimika children had been leaving—as Johannas, their houseboy, did for Bible school—the Mimikas would mourn them as though dead, groaning and wailing and wallowing in the mud along the riverbank. They mourned what the spirits might do to the relative far away where they could not see him. It was common for tribal members to be kidnapped by other tribes and never be seen again. How did they know whether or not people who left the village in an airplane would ever come back?

So the Rascher farewell was on display. They must do it *not as people without hope.* They must show that they had another Source of strength that let them say goodbye and not fear the beyond. The attitude was easy. But the hugs, the kisses, the prayers for each other were difficult with two thousand staring black eyes.

Pilot Clell Rogers taxied up the river in an empty float plane to pick up the Rascher kids. At Jawsakor they would switch to a plane without floats and be joined by children from other south coast stations. These plane rides were the only times the kids wore sweaters, except at annual conferences in the mountains.

The children were strapped in on laps and sometimes laps upon laps to fly up, up over the interior mountains and down into Sentani on the north coast. The biggest kids sat up front with the pilot—what a privilege! Chip was the smallest and was strapped on top of the suitcases.

There was a gleeful claustrophobia that the children would always associate with leaving for school. The ride was like Disneyland. The pilots were heroes.

Out the little windows was a dense, dark-green world: the jungle. Its wildness, its mystery, even its oppressive heat lost their omnipotence from the air. The children could look at it in wonder—free, detached from its influence.

Everywhere below was aglitter from standing water in the swamps. As they climbed inland, the shimmer was from countless waterfalls and churning rivers.

The pilots in the pioneering stages of missionary work in West Irian were a different breed. That's not to say that safety wasn't their primary concern. They were seasoned pilots used to flying in all weather conditions and with a healthy respect for danger. Pilot Clell Rogers, for example, was well aware of the precious nature of his cargo to Sentani. But, well, if the kids all kept rocking the plane together, if they *insisted* he do it, well, Clell had to let the plane take a roll. Just a few times.

Clell liked to see that his passengers were both safely transported and enjoyed their trip. On one flight, when only the Rascher family was aboard and the children were small, Clell played his trumpet while flying the plane to help Chip take his nap.

Meanwhile in Kokonao, Larry and Shirley and little Gregory ate and took a nap, following routine as much as they could. But then there was the waking up. The house was so still. The work of many days was completed, but without satisfaction.

Gregory toddled from room to room, knowing that his brothers and sister were gone but not knowing why the house felt so strange. Gone was the smell of earth, and play, and sweaty little bodies. And the noises: "Mom!" "Hey, Dad. . . ." The squabbling and the laughter. The life that young bodies exude and that older bodies long to soak in.

The big kids might cry at night a few times in Sentani, but the longer crying on the inside would belong to Larry and Shirley.

The northern coast of West Irian was entirely different

from the mucky swamplands of the south coast. Mountains trailed their skirts gently down to the ocean. The beaches were fine white sand or coral. The Sentani School of the Christian and Missionary Alliance was at the base of a mountain which sat between the school and the coast. Jayapura, the capital city, lay over a narrow mountain road to the east; huge Lake Sentani was to the south; there was an MAF base between the lake and the school.

The children of Sentani School knew each of these landmarks. One Saturday a month they traveled by bus to Jayapura to shop for little balloons to blow up with plastic straws, and for cheese curls, candy and other special items. Eventually the *tokos* sold gum, which was gold. Grandma Rascher once sent Keith a package of gum. Keith kept the chewed wad on his bedpost and used it over and over for weeks. Eventually he sold it to a friend.

On semester break the students were taken for a boat ride and swimming on Lake Sentani. And they spent many of their Friday Fun Nights roller skating in the hangar at the MAF base.

There were about eighty students in grades one through eight, living in one rambling dormitory building and later in hostels built by each of the missions from which children came. Each mission also had a guest house where parents could stay and be with their children. Larry and Shirley came for their vacations— two weeks in the fall and two in the spring—and the children came home to Kokonao for a month at Christmas and two-and-a-half months in the summer. The family was never apart for more than two months at a time.

The academic standards were high at Sentani and the facilities were very adequate. The school was famous for its band, in which all the children played. All American holidays were celebrated, sometimes with an

Irian twist, such as a pig feast for Thanksgiving.

In elementary school Kathy Rascher was a bit taller than average with short blond hair, glasses, and a thoroughly unaffected, sweet smile. She was a head taller than Keith through elementary school, but Keith was too busy to be much concerned about it. Kathy got along with everyone.

Kathy loved school, especially art class. She worked hard on the extra things: her science projects, her Halloween costumes, practicing the piano. She made A's and competed with Brent Preston for top grades in their class of six students.

Since her class was very small, Kathy played with girls older and younger than she, who looked up to her. They rode their bikes, played tether ball, and made pottery out of red clay from a hill nearby. With a neighborhood so full of kids, there were continuous games of kickball, Red Rover, and Prisoner's Base. On rainy days the kids worked on collections: stamps, rubber bands, lead, marbles, baseball cards.

Kathy mothered her brothers as much as they'd stand for, and her mandatory Sunday letters home were newsy and kept her parents up-to-date on both her own doings and those of the boys.

Everyone who knew them said the Rascher boys were not bad kids. Their pranks were notorious, but never malicious. They stretched the expression "all boy."

Perhaps it was harder on Mr. Hazlett, their new teacher and principal, that the boys were tender-hearted. Discipline became a matter of grays when the misbehavior was taken "in fun."

When Mr. Hazlett came, Keith and Kathy were in his fifth grade class. He also taught sixth and seventh grades in the same room for a total of twenty-one students.

Because school was also home, and because the school was relatively new and there were not yet many rules on the books, the kids at Sentani, particularly Keith and his buddies Brent Preston and Buzzy Maxey, felt proprietary about "the way things were done." After all, they *liked* the way things were done. They tried to explain these precedents to Mr. Hazlett, who had to convince them that he was the teacher and principal, and that things could change. Consequently, many ensuing school rules could have been named in honor of this trio.

Until they did it, no one had thought of spinning kids in the hand-operated cement mixer down by the swimming pool construction site. Or of playing Robin Hood soccer using stick "cudgels" instead of feet. Or of laying poles across ditches so you could ride your bike across them when being chased. Or of shooting birds with slingshots.

Before these boys, no one had played bicycle tag so hard at recess that they sweated pools on the classroom floor and couldn't write because their papers got so wet. "No bicycles at recess" was decreed.

Each of these activities was "disallowed," with good reason, as dangerous. But of course each new rule merely challenged the boys' imaginations. They had to have something to do.

To be fair, who do you suppose Mr. Hazlett's wife, Mary, called to remove a large lizard that had wandered into her second grade classroom? And what fellows were the hardest workers helping a native work crew dig and construct the school swimming pool?

Chip learned from his older brother. Adults saw Chip as a quiet, slight child, blond and freckled and extremely likeable. But by seventh and eighth grade Chip had surpassed Keith's antics at Sentani. His favorite was swinging on a cable, as the "Flying Fox," from the second floor of the TEAM hostel construction site to the ground. He loved to hook up the dorm generator in the middle of the night so the lights came on.

The environs of Sentani did not deter boys with a creative bent. The school was on the site of General MacArthur's Post 7 of World War II in the Pacific. The old mess hall was still standing. The Regions Beyond Missionary Union guest house was in an army Quonset. Slabs from barracks checkered the campus.

Relics of war littered about were ammunition for boys' dreams: a machine gun on a tripod, mortar launchers, helmets, rusting vehicles. Such things were found all along the north shores of New Guinea, where roadside beautification is of absolutely no concern.

Buzzy, Brent and Keith—and Chip and his friends after—saw treasure in bullets and old batteries, which they melted down for the lead. Lead became the school currency. Pieces were collected by the boys and traded by boys and girls. At vacation the boys' suitcases came home full of lead for fishing weights and for trading with the natives. They were also full of rocks for sling-shots (hard to find in the swamps), bicycle tubes and marbles.

"Aunt" Pat Fillmore was a school nurse at Sentani who took diligent care of each student. Anything red—a scrape, a cut—must be soaked with clean, hot water to prevent infection. In the tropics sores fester within twenty-four hours. Each afternoon students sat in rows outside the clinic with cans of steaming water and washcloths to "soak" their sores. The Rascher kids put in their time.

One day Pat saw Chip hobbling down the hall to class and asked him what was wrong.

"Oh, nothing. I've just got a bad case of jungle rot [athlete's foot] and my shoes are too tight." Pat ordered Chip to sit down and take off his shoes and socks. Shoes were required in school, which was about the only time some of these kids wore them.

It was a sad sight. She couldn't see how he could bare to wedge his feet into his shoes.

"You leave those shoes off and meet me this afternoon at the clinic. I'll send a note to Mr. Hazlett that says you need to have them off, and we'll start soaks and meds this afternoon." Chip grinned at Pat and ran on to class with shoes and socks in hand.

Aunt Pat was in charge one day when Chip came to her to show off his trophy. He had melted all kinds of bullets and made a dandy ball of lead. She was appalled, but thankful Chip stood before her without burns and alive. The house parents were off that day and she was in charge of all the students, plus the clinic, plus the dining room. She was in no mood to deal with a medical emergency and tried to squelch the melting of lead. But the business thrived underground, in the jungle just off campus.

The boys smashed batteries, gathered bullets and melted the lead into rectangular bricks over a fire using kitchen match boxes for molds. Sometimes they used plastic molding from old batteries. When these were damp the hot lead exploded and burned the boys, fortunately never too seriously.

The practice died suddenly. Brent had offered to buy Buzzy's watch for seventy blocks of lead. Buzzy couldn't believe his windfall and agreed. Brent had not specified what size blocks, however, and cut up seventy miniature blocks to give to Buzzy. The currency was devalued by the episode. The boys lost interest.

When Larry and Shirley went to Sentani on vacation it was a two-week celebration of "together-life." The children got to stay in the guest house with their parents and Gregory, eating together and going back and forth to class. Each of the kids had his or her own life at school and didn't cling to the folks for those two weeks. But they were proud of their parents and liked to have their friends over.

Larry was a popular dad with the Sentani kids because he joined in their tag and soccer games. They thought he was a bit long-winded when he preached at the school's weekly chapel services. But that was okay. The kids could tell he cared about them a lot.

Shirley made a point of looking up friends' children at school to see how they were doing and to mother them a little.

Dinner time was the best. Each of them had weeks of living to tell the others about. Shirley's cooking was best when many chairs were filled around the table.

"Guess what Brent Preston gave me," Kathy began one night with a pleased grin.

Chip rolled his eyes, "They make me deliver their notes for them." Brent didn't give all his attention to Keith and Buzzy.

"Brent gave me a blue ring," she continued. "It was plastic, all in one piece and it sort of bubbled out in the front. It was really pretty."

"Where is it?" asked Shirley. "Did you give it back to him?"

"Oh, no. But one day I had it off in class to look at it and I accidentally dropped it down the metal pipe that holds the top of my desk to the bottom." Kathy's eyes got big and round.

Keith and Chip laughed—exaggerated laughter which irritated Kathy. "It's not funny!" she said.

"Well, what did you do?" Shirley asked.

"I just make sure that when I'm around Brent he can't see it's not on my hand."

"What did you two talk about that day he asked you to meet him at the red dirt?" Chip asked.

"How did you know about that? I thought you didn't read the notes!"

"So what if I do, if I don't tell anyone. But you didn't go, did you?"

"Of course I didn't go!" She and Brent never actually talked *to* each other—too embarrassing!

"Boys," said Larry, who paused to look at them

seriously over a couple of bites of dinner. "The principal talked to me today. It's one thing to have fun, but it sounds like you've been destructive. That doesn't sound like you guys. I want you to tell us what happened."

"Oh, you mean the ceiling tag?" asked Keith.

"Ceiling tag?" Larry looked across at Shirley and chuckled in spite of himself, then regained his composure. "Yes, tell us about the ceiling tag."

"Sunday afternoons are so boring, Dad," Keith began. The dorm parents and teachers all have a meeting so they make us take naps. Can you see us lyin' there with our hands folded?

"You know how those ceilings are just quarter-inch sheets of asbestos? Well, you can run the rafters in the attic. It's hot as blazes, so we don't do it very often.

"But Sunday afternoon we were playing hide-and-seek in the dorm and Chip and I and some guys got up there through the crawl space. We were running the rafters up there when someone yelled, 'Uncle Frank's coming!' I fell straight through the ceiling and landed on all fours right in front of the guy. You should have seen the look on his face!" They all laughed heartily, forgetting for a moment the hole in the ceiling.

"And here were all these sweaty faces peering down at Uncle Frank and me through the hole."

"I hid up in the attic behind the suitcases until dinner time. Man, I thought I'd sweat to death," said Chip.

"Mr. Hazlett says the ceiling has been fixed, but did you apologize to him?" Larry asked.

"Yes, and I did punishment two Saturday mornings— any chores Uncle Frank wanted me to do."

Shirley and Kathy cleared the table, scraping and rinsing the dishes and taking the garbage out back away from the ants. Shirley lit the Petromax lamp in the center of the table and poured more iced tea. Outside, darkness had come abruptly. Little lizards scoured the walls and ceiling for mosquitoes. No one was in a hurry to leave the table.

"I hear you were lost in the swamp again, Dad," said Keith. "Mr. Hazlett told us, 'Now don't be worried, but they can't find your dad.'"

"Margaret came over that Sunday morning while Larry was missing so we could have our own church service by the radio," said Shirley. "We were singing morbid choruses." Shirley's laughter joined Keith's.

"But did you think he really wouldn't come back, Mom?" Kathy asked.

"No, somehow the Lord gave me peace that he would." Shirley didn't worry when Larry was away. Not since the first time he'd left to patrol with Harold Lovestrand in Kokonao when she was alone with three young children and laid awake listening to the jungle cheeps and chatters in the night. She was frightened then because it was all new and she hadn't expected this to be part of the job. Now she accepted it. When missionary wives were afraid—or simply wanted some companionship—they would often stay on another mission station while their husbands were away. Sometimes Shirley did that.

"I wasn't worried either. I always figure Dad will show up somewhere," said Keith.

"Me, too," said Kathy, but she had worried about when they would find him, and she had looked at her family photograph often and prayed for him. Kathy thought the world of her dad.

"Well," began Larry, "Hekman and I wondered for a while. Bill and I were in an old thirty-foot metal Motor Moppi hauling a load of lumber from Kokonao to the sawmill at Agats.

"We had packed on the two-ton limit. Those tubs never were very seaworthy.

"We meant to go most of the way by ocean, but, man, it was so choppy that we knew we couldn't make it loaded down like we were.

"We went in at a river mouth, but the tide was going out and we knew real soon that this river wasn't going to get us anywhere.

"Some Asmaters were bivouacked in there. I mean to tell you there was nothing but knee-deep mud, but they'd thrown together some palm leaves to make a kind of teepee. Hekman can speak some of their dialect of Asmat, and they showed him a cut-through, just a little creek they said we could get through at high tide over to a larger river.

"'They've gotta be kiddin', I said to Hekman. The creek was fifteen feet wide at the mouth and the boat was eight or nine feet wide.

"They said, 'When the water covers that log, it will be deep enough.' We're talkin' six or eight feet deep when it covered the log. The boat needed four or five feet of water to float.

"It sounded like *omong kosong*, empty talk, but we didn't have any better ideas, so we went into the creek when the tide came up. Only we blinked and the tide had gone out again. I've never seen it come and go so fast. The water fed back out the creek to both sides leaving us grounded in low water and mud in the middle.

"Here we were," Larry said, his hands telling the story, "stuck in the swamp where no one knew to look for us. We'd said we were going by ocean."

"Couldn't that long white canopy on the boat be seen from the air?" asked Chip.

"Sure it could on the ocean, but where we were the jungle roof was too thick. In fact, we heard Hoisington fly over not twenty feet above us, but he must not have seen us."

"What about the radio?" asked Kathy.

"That was the biggest problem," said Larry. "We couldn't transmit anything. We could hear on it plain as anything. We heard Verena Hekman calling MAF for help. We were supposed to check in with the girls on the radio each day at 10:00 a.m. and 1:00 p.m. Verena got worried when we didn't check in either time. We could hear her and Shirley talking it over on the radio. We could hear MAF dispatching all their planes to look for us. And here we were pushing this tub full of lumber through the mud!

"We could tell by walking along the bank that the worst part lasted about a block. We pushed the boat that far until the tide came back in. Even then we had to push to get her out to the river at the other end. We spent the whole day in a three or four mile creek.

"The next day Clell Rogers spotted us from the single engine Cessna. We could hear him on the radio: 'I've got a target. Normal operation. Third river over.' He threw a roll of toilet paper which nearly hit the canopy to mark where we were and sort of let us know he was thinking of our welfare.

"Then Dave Hoisington flew in and landed the float plane. We sure felt sheepish. 'Dave,' I said, 'we sure feel sorry for all the trouble for everybody. We were stuck and couldn't get the radio working.'

"We had taken the top off the radio, but we couldn't figure out what to do with it. Hoisington tinkered with it a minute. He stripped a wire and put it back in. He said the coaxial cable had shorted at the radio. He tried it: 'Do you copy, Jawsakor?'

"'Loud and clear, Motor Moppi!' It worked fine first try."

Larry was leaning on his elbows at the table in his T-shirt and shorts. "That's all there was to it. Man, were we embarrassed! Hoisington rubbed it in, too."

"We got the boat out of there and worked our way along the rivers. That was Sunday afternoon. That night we grounded on a sandbar and the motor conked out on us."

"Did you fix it?" Chip asked.

"You'd better believe we did. No way were we going to call for help!"

In March of the year Kathy and Keith were eleven years old and in the sixth grade at Sentani, Kathy was playing volleyball after school. In the middle of play—she was watching the ball intently—a note was passed to her. She stopped the game so she could read it. "You have a new baby sister: Karen Joyce Rascher." Kathy jumped and yelled and skipped around, showing her friends. A baby sister. A baby sister! The world belonged to Kathy.

In her first letter to Kathy after the birth, Shirley sent the traced outline of Karen's tiny foot. Karen was a five-pound baby, petite but perfectly formed. Kathy sent back a tracing of her own foot for Karen.

It was always hard to get to sleep the night before the kids went home for summer vacation—like the night before Christmas. This year was the worst for Kathy.

The boarding students at Sentani were all up before dawn and were driven with their luggage to the MAF base. With the first light the first load of children was on its way home.

When the Cessna neared Kokonao, Kathy peered out the tiny window. As they taxied to a stop at the bank she could see her mom and dad, chubby little Greg, and a gaggle of natives. Where was her baby sister? Did she really have one? Was it just a dream? Had something happened?

Karen had been sleeping, so Shirley had left her at home with the house helper. As Kathy walked into her room there was the crib—in her room! Karen was asleep in just a diaper with her bottom in the air, and Kathy loved her immediately with all her heart.

CONTACT

The Raschers had lived six years in Kokonao when God ordained an amazing match.

The matchmaker was Korwa, a male nurse who had been transferred from the Catholic hospital in Kokonao to remote Akimuga. Larry suspected Korwa had been transferred because he was a leader in the Kokonao TEAM church.

In Akimuga Korwa befriended Nafaripi tribesmen who had heard through the jungle grapevine of the nurse at Akimuga, and had come for medical care. Korwa liked them. He began to learn their language. Esapa, a Nafaripi chief, gave Korwa two boys to raise in Akimuga with the stipulation that Korwa teach them to speak Indonesian. Communication had begun.

Korwa told the Nafaripi he knew how they could get a teacher and a school for their tribe. He began to tell them about a living God who loved them.

The Nafaripi asked Korwa to patrol their rivers and treat their people. They were nomads, living in clans which moved along "their" rivers in the swamps wherever fishing or crocodile hunting or sago gathering was best or their enemies sparcest. Whole families moved along the rivers in dugout canoes: dogs in front, then implements, and people in the back. The men stood in the back to paddle with long pole-like oars.

They were a small tribe, numbering only a few hundred. They had to be particularly ferocious and move often to deter attacks from larger, neighboring tribes.

Larry and Shirley had once seen some Nafaripi. On Independence Day one August a clan came to Kokonao for the festivities. They came with bows and arrows, so they were left to themselves and kept to themselves, camping in the Raschers' front yard.

The men were muscular from chopping trees with axes and paddling canoes. All were nearly naked, except for one man who had taken a blouse of Shirley's from the clothesline. It was a good one with a matching skirt, so she told him she wanted it back and he gave it to her.

It was a curious scene, almost like a portrait painted for the Raschers, with their front window as its frame. They still believed it was for people such as these that they had come to West Irian. Larry and Shirley had begun to pray that the Lord would come into the lives of the Nafaripi.

Korwa and Larry corresponded, arranging a rendezvous between Larry and Nafaripi leaders. On the designated date Larry had been at the right spot on the Cemara River; he saw no one.

Now they were trying again. Larry, fellow missionary Jim Hyatt, and three Asmat tribesmen were idling up the Cemara in TEAM's inboard diesel Motor Moppi with a load of lumber for the station at Amar. The canvas side curtains flapped idly. The men peered into the dark green wall of vegetation beyond gnarled roots on either bank. There was no one. Larry was frustrated and heartbroken. Couldn't he even depend on Korwa?

In fact, Korwa and twenty Nafaripi had only a day earlier given up on the meeting and left. They had bivouacked on the river two weeks early so they wouldn't miss the *tuan*. The moon was full so the mosquitoes were atrocious. The tides had been high so the fishing was poor. Natives are impatient by nature. How did they know Korwa had really talked to the *tuan*? Why should they think he was really coming? They had lost track of the time and had given up.

Jim Hyatt looked at the contorted lines on their map of the south coast. They were sure they had counted the river mouths correctly. Larry pounded his fist on the steering wheel, and scanned the brown river for a spot to turn his load around.

"Look, *Tuan*, look!" called an Asmater. Tied to a pole in the middle of the river was a note in a plastic bag. Of course a native had found it; Larry admired their keenness. It was from Korwa. "We have left but go on up. Take first main river on right. You will find some Nafaripi there."

Larry gave a whoop and nudged the throttle. This was what he and Shirley had longed for. *I hope Korwa is right*, he thought, as the tide got lower and lower, for further up river sandbars and the gathering darkness would make navigation testy. Soon they would have to drop anchor for the night.

Around a bend sat a huddle of palm-leaf huts on the mud of the riverbank. As the boat approached it, the women and children fled into the jungle. Five grinning natives were bold enough to greet them at the bank. None of them looked to be war chiefs or anyone of importance. They knew no Indonesian, but smiled and gestured. They seemed intent upon convincing the *tuans* that they really had many people, not a few, on up the river.

Larry and Jim joined the little band at their fire. The natives had a whole pile of roasted sago worms. They handed the *tuans* fifteen, poked onto a skewer. Jim had eaten grubs before—but Jim would eat anything. Larry had had a few when hospitality demanded it. Over the teeth and through the gums. . . . This was certainly no time to offend. Conversation wasn't a promising option and there wasn't much to do but eat grubs. It was about 9:00 p.m. when they began eating with expressions of appreciation.

The grubs resemble marshmallows. They taste like bacon, only fattier. Grubs are a jungle treat: a chocolate sundae.

Within an hour Larry was in trouble. Red welts rose all over his body and he itched like crazy. He took off his T-shirt and Jim helped him scratch. His face and eyes were swollen and his trachea had nearly closed. Fear made his breathing come harder.

Jim got the radio out of the boat and reached Dr. Dresser in Pirimapun. The doctor had Jim check the medications they carried in the boat. They had aspirin, but no antihistamine. No float plane could bring them any in the jungle in the middle of the night. For a couple of hours, until the reaction peaked and subsided, Larry thought he was gone.

Morning found the two alive but tired and queasy. They continued as far up-river as the boat could go, with some Nafaripi as eager motorboat passengers, to greet all of the tribe they could find.

When Larry returned home he sent word to Korwa. "If the Nafaripi want us to come, you must get me an official invitation to show the government officials." Korwa responded with a document which, when it arrived by boat from Akimuga, sent a chill down Larry's sweaty spine. Larry held a letter written in Korwa's hand which read "We would like to have the missionary of TEAM to come among us and teach us the Bible." It was signed with the inky thumb-prints of the chiefs of the Nafaripi: nomads, cannibals.

The Nafaripi, Korwa and Larry chose a site for the Nafaripi village of Sumapero. Larry sent word to Korwa to have the Nafaripi wait for him there on a certain day. Larry flew to the site in a float plane with the *Camat*, or head government official from Kokonao, and a policeman. Six *atap,* palm-leaf shingled houses were in place when they arrived. Perhaps a hundred Nafaripi men met them at the bank.

The Nafaripi met with the delegation in a hastily constructed man's house, where the single and widowed men of a clan would live.

Korwa and the two Nafaripi boys he had been raising interpreted for them. First the *Camat* extended a formal greeting to the tribesmen, intimidatingly wild men, and powerfully built. Then he asked, "Do you want these missionaries to come and stay here? Do you want to have a school for your children?"

Larry spoke before they answered. He was intent that they understand what he was proposing to them, so he repeated it several times, pausing for the interpreters and watching for signs of comprehension. "We are not coming to bring you machetes and axes and things you want. You must understand that. We are not coming to give you things. We would come to tell you about the God who created heaven and earth and who loves you. You should want to know about Him and we would come to tell you. We would like to live with you and help you build a school and find teachers. But in order for your children to go to school you must settle in this village and not just move along the rivers. My family will need a place to live, too.

"Now I'm going to ask you this," Larry concluded. "How many of you are interested in having God's Son come into your lives? In putting away evil spirits? How many of you want school for your children? I need to know how many of you want us to come."

As Larry finished talking, the Nafaripi huddled briefly. The atmosphere of the room was oppressive with heat and the smell of sweat and smoke and with tense anticipation. Larry longed to step outside, but he waited. He wished he could understand their language. Presently the talk ended and these strong, nearly-naked men moved en masse to the far side of the room.

It took Larry a few moments to understand what they were saying to him. It took months for him to understand its significance. They were saying, "Yes, we all want this. You come." Some men consented, perhaps, only because their clan leaders had. That didn't matter. The statement had been made by three clans of the Nafaripi tribe: the Waitiko, the Epeme, and the Wumani. Bands of ignorance, superstition and revenge which had bound them tight for thousands of years in the swamps were now unbuckled.

SUMAPERO

Sumapero was a point of high ground where a cutoff river and the Cemara River joined. Those who lived on the south coast of West Irian knew mud from mud. They would say the mud at Sumapero was the slimiest, the gooiest, the worst. At low tide it lay exposed to the sunlight exuding its own particular stench.

When MAF pilot George Boggs left Larry and Shirley there or brought them supplies, he didn't linger. He sensed Satanic spirits and saw a ferociousness in the faces of the people. The largest crocodile head he'd ever seen greeted him on a stump near the river, half decayed. It did not seem welcoming to George.

Larry and Shirley saw it otherwise when they came to Sumapero with their toddler son and Shirley pregnant in late 1968. They were met at the shore by excited Nafaripi who carried the *tuans'* supplies to the *atap* house constructed for them. Shirley didn't care what the place looked or smelled like. In Kokonao they had been outcasts and felt unwanted. Here the Nafaripi took them in as family. They were all embarking upon the adventure of village life together. This would be home. They would live here and periodically visit Kokonao to check on the work among the Mimikas.

Their house was built twice the size of a native house which sheltered ten to twelve people. It was perched on four-foot stilts, with steps to the front door and a plank walkway from the back door to the cookhouse and the outhouse. The Raschers placed barrels along the walkway to catch rainwater for drinking.

They soon learned they had to remove the steps at night. They were the only ones in the village who stored food, who kept on hand more than was needed for one day. This made their home attractive to all the mangy, nearly furless village dogs, who were kept hungry to make them better hunters.

Korwa, the nurse, had been transferred to a government hospital in the mountains of the interior, and they would never see him again in Sumapero. But before he left, Korwa had planted marigolds in front of the Rascher house and corn beside it. Behind the house lofty ironwood trees formed a barrier: *Your civilization may go this far, no farther.*

To Larry and Shirley the house was perfect, except in one respect.

At first Larry communicated with the Nafaripi through the two Nafaripi boys whom Korwa had taught Indonesian, and through sign language, at which he was adept. The language of the Nafaripi was ironically a combination of Mimika and Asmat tongues. Larry and Shirley had lived with Mimikas at Kokonao, and with Asmaters at Pirimapun. They had had good preparation for tackling the language of the people of Sumapero.

Larry asked the two boys who spoke Indonesian the Nafaripi word for *windows*. They said there was none. The Indonesian word brought blank looks from the natives. Larry pretended to whack at the wall of their house with a machete.

"Do you want holes in the sides of the house?" asked Esapa, chief of the Waitiko clan, who lived next door with his five wives. "Yes," said Larry. "Four holes: here, here, there, and there."

"But it will rain in," protested Esapa.

"Not if we bring the edge of the roof out farther."

"But how will you keep warm at night? You do not have a fire within your house as we do."

"We will use cloth to cover us," Larry replied.

The *tuans* were hard to please, the natives thought. But they chopped windows for the Raschers, then chopped them in their own houses as well.

The village of Sumapero sprang up quickly. Korwa and Larry both had a hand in laying out the village on the highest ground they could find on a wide bend of the river. The village had a path down the center. Waitiko clan houses were on one side and Epeme clan houses on the other. Wumani clan, former enemies of Waitiko, lived in a cluster of houses at one end of the village. The Rascher house was at the other end. Each Nafaripi house sheltered a man, his wives and their children. Larry helped build special houses for each clan's chief.

In addition, each clan had its own man's house where no women were allowed. There decisions were made and the old men beat the drums and told stories. There were no jails in these villages. Matters were settled in the man's house.

There were perhaps 300 to 350 Nafaripi living in Sumapero at any one time. The numbers fluctuated because of the old influence of nomadic living.

The village had an initiation house with elaborate carvings, for the boys' rites of passage into manhood.

Moses and Benoni came from Kokonao to serve as school teachers. They and the Nafaripi children constructed a school/church building of *atap*. Larry had little Nafaripi boys following him wherever he went. "Hey, what's your name?" he asked each one, squatting to talk to him.

"Asu," said one boy of about four years of age.

"Asu," said another.

"I'm Asu," asserted a third little fellow.

At first Larry thought they were teasing him. But the boys seemed serious enough.

"Why are they all named Asu?" Larry asked his two young interpreters. "There are others as well," they said. "They are named for the Waitiko warrior Asu. He was our greatest warrior and our enemies were afraid of him." Asu had an ulcerated tooth, as the story went. His mouth became grotesquely swollen. The pain confined him to his mat in his house.

The clan of Wumani, then enemies of Waitiko, heard of Asu's toothache. One night they surrounded his house and fired volleys of arrows through the *atap*. Asu and his favorite wife were killed. If he had not been so ill he would have killed many of his attackers, the boys assured Larry. A second wife escaped into the jungle. The third wife and her two daughters were captured, killed and eaten.

Boys born after that were named Asu until revenge was taken and someone was killed in Wumani. Now clan members of Waitiko and Wumani were making a tenuous attempt to live in a village together with the *tuans* at Sumapero. Since Sumapero sat on the Waitiko's river, they were having to share their rights to the sago found along it. It occurred to Larry that nearly everyone in their village had surely eaten human flesh.

The chief in Sumapero, recognized as leader over all three clans, was Esapa. Chip Rascher was in awe from his first sight of the man. Larry was proud to have such a neighbor and friend.

Esapa was tall, strong, and handsome. His large nose had a hole where he'd once worn a nose bone. Now he wore no decorations except a headdress of yellow cockatoo feathers for village feasts. He didn't need any. His appearance and bearing were regal. Esapa decided what the whole tribe would do: whether they would hunt or fish or weave mats on any given day. From his leadership his people took security and identity.

Esapa was known throughout the swamps as a fierce warrior who had killed many. But he wore no boar tusks on his arms to show how many he had killed, and Larry saw in his neighbor's eyes no hint of the wild look of some Nafaripi. He saw the intelligence which had meant survival for Esapa's tribe. He was the best hunter, the best fisherman, the best warrior. He could make decisions. At around forty years of age, he was in his prime. He was first to say of Christianity "We want it." He said to his people, "We will attend the *tuan's* church."

Sunday services commenced immediately and were a terrific challenge for Larry. To say something relevant to their lives . . . to say something understandable to them in their language or in Indonesian . . . to find illustrations that would fit in their culture . . . to find humor that would be funny to them . . . Larry had his hands full.

It was in his favor that the people were used to listening to stories and would pay attention if the speaker was loud and animated. If anyone could be loud and animated, it was Larry Rascher.

Larry wrestled with how to adapt Bible truths to a context relevant to the Nafaripi. One Sunday he took a cup. The Nafaripi didn't have many cups yet, but they were a popular trade item. Larry walked to the river before the service and filled the cup with the murky water that the Nafaripi used for cooking and bathing.

"There's no way I can put clean water into this till I pour out the dirty water," Larry said to the gathered Nafaripi, as he slowly poured the brown water onto the church's dirt floor.

Then he took one of the bamboo tubes which the people used to collect rain water for drinking, and he filled his aluminum cup. He talked to them about repentance. They needed to empty themselves of the bad inside them so that God could fill them with the good.

That night as Larry and Shirley sat talking after Greg was in bed, as the villagers sat around their fires in their houses eating roasted sago or fish, they heard a man yelling in the center of the village. They recognized Esapa's voice. Larry and Shirley listened at their screen door. Esapa ranted on and on, haranguing the women of the village for their lazy ways. "The men are hungry," he yelled. "You need to get up earlier and get sago."

When Esapa finished with the women, he chastised the conduct of the men.

"He keeps saying 'Moke! Moke!' What does that mean?" Larry asked their Nafaripi houseboy.

"It means 'cup.' *Boppa,* he is preaching your sermon."

They listened in amazement. When Esapa finished, other men and women took their turns expounding from the center of the village.

"It's all wrong on Sunday morning, isn't it Shirley?" Larry asked.

"Yes, when they're usually hunting or fishing," she said.

"And sitting on those benches instead of around their fires. This is when they talk about important things."

"Yes," Shirley mused.

The *tuans* were learning, as were the Nafaripi. Often Esapa would re-preach Larry's sermons at night when the people were settled. And when fighting broke out in the village—usually two women at each other with machetes or logs—Esapa would come to Larry. "*Tuan,* come help us. They are causing great sin."

The Nafaripi sang. They sang to tell stories, to chronicle events, to pass on traditions, to mourn, to celebrate. But the music was spontaneous, tonal, sing-song, chanted to a lizard-skin drum beat. The Nafaripi children began to learn Indonesian songs in school. They sang these songs in church and the adults mumbled an accompanying chant.

School was taught in Indonesian, which the children learned quickly. The teachers had the only books—basic primers—and a large blackboard, a piece of 4 x 8 plywood which Larry painted with blackboard paint. Each student was provided a government-issue slate. Subjects were taught by rote, sums and sentences recited over and over in unison. The adults couldn't help but learn also if they lived anywhere near the school. After Larry built homes for the village chiefs, he constructed a big school house on ironwood stilts.

To learn the Nafaripi language, Larry spent mornings with native language helpers going over word lists. Shirley took her babies with her and visited with the village women at their chores. She walked through the village with a walking stick to ward off resident pigs, who snorted at humans and sometimes attacked. But the Nafaripi were quick to put their pigs inside when they saw *tuans* coming, for fear the pigs would be a nuisance.

Esapa's favorite wife, as befitting her position, took Shirley under her wing. She came around in the mornings to see what help Shirley needed. She brought her sago, fish or meat. She saved Shirley a seat in church.

The villagers shared with one another to a degree the Raschers had not seen in West Irian. If a family had taken their canoe into the swamps and returned a few days later with sago, they would distribute it to others. Fish, crocodiles and vegetables from their gardens in the jungle were shared. Most mornings Shirley would find bricks of sago on the back porch, or a bunch of bananas.

Larry and Shirley loved these people who had so totally adopted them. They enjoyed their personalities. They relished being in the center of a work where the Holy Spirit was moving and active.

They knew change was inevitable and accelerated

for these stone-age people who had bumped into a twentieth century American family in their swamps. They wanted to help ensure the changes were for the better. They did not want to superimpose their own culture upon the Nafaripi.

Certainly many Nafaripi ways were inconsistent with those of a believer in Jesus Christ. But Larry and Shirley believed that as they taught the people God's Word, these matters would come to the natives' attention. The Nafaripi could then find their own solutions.

Larry and Shirley refused to allow the natives to begin asking them for things. If a native had nothing suitable as payment for the goods he requested, Larry would at least create a job so he could earn them. Once when Keith, Kathy and Chip were home from Sentani for the summer, a native man came to Larry and asked him for a fish hook. "I don't have a hook, *Tuan,* and I need to go fishing." Larry wanted the man to be able to fish, but the man had nothing to trade. Larry knew if he let one man get by, others would come asking.

Keith, home on school vacation, overheard the conversation. He felt sorry for the man and intercepted him coming around the corner of the house empty-handed. Keith held out some Monopoly money. "Here," he said, grinning. "You give this to *Bapak* and he'll give you a fish hook." Which he did.

While not wanting to destroy their culture, at the same time Larry was constantly hunting ways to help the people better their existence. If his ideas sometimes boomeranged, if they were occasionally cultural bloopers, they at least came with the best of intentions. Besides *living,* plus building for TEAM Irian, preaching, studying the language and manning stations at both Kokonao and Sumapero took a lot of time. There wasn't much left over for the study of the culture—assuming that the natives even wanted to tell them why they believed and did things as they did—which they usually didn't. The language barrier made it difficult for the Nafaripi to explain their culture. And Larry and Shirley assumed that the culture would continue the same and that they could catch "what that meant" the next time it came up.

Two of Larry's ideas of mixed value were chickens and coconut trees. The arrival of the chickens was a big event. The people gathered around, excited. Larry divided the chickens between the clans and his own family. But the chickens were so afraid of the village dogs that they roosted on the rooftops at night. Eggs were laid willy-nilly in the village. The Nafaripi would rather trade the eggs than eat them, so they brought them to the Raschers.

Larry brought coconut trees by boat from Kokonao. He and the natives planted saplings along the walkway from the dock to the village. The rest he divided between clan chiefs and his own family. He made the mistake, however, of paying natives to dig the holes and plant the trees in his yard. To them the planting of a tree meant possession of it, so the Raschers' trees were often stripped of coconuts.

Larry hired men to build a bed frame with bamboo slats tied in with rattan. A bed was a novelty. Every man in Sumapero had to have one. One night, a man was sleeping on his woven mat atop his new bed with one of his wives. His other wife slept by the fire on the floor. In the night the entire village was awakened by the screams of the wife by the fire. A twenty-foot python was coiled around her. The husband saved his wife by chopping the snake to pieces with his machete. Later the natives ate the snake. Unfortunately, chickens attracted pythons.

When a native died in Sumapero, Larry encouraged the practice, new to the natives, of burying their dead instead of mounting them on racks to rot in the sun. The idea seemed sound enough. But Larry discovered the water table was so high that the first body he buried began floating to the surface before it could be covered with dirt. He had to wedge it down with sticks. Larry looked for higher ground for future burials.

When the older Rascher kids were home in Sumapero on school vacations, family life had a wonderful simplicity. They played with native friends till past dark—Prisoner's Base or Kick the Can. Kathy often played with the boys because Nafaripi girls her age were married, or nearly so.

The Raschers had an electric generator, but fuel was scarce. Instead of using it they generally lit the Petromax lamp, the Indonesian version of a Coleman lantern, and let its light draw them together, while dark eyes watched them through the window screens. They played Monopoly or Aggravation or Sorry under the lamp. Often Shirley and Kathy put the little ones to bed and played Scrabble while they waited up for Larry, Keith and Chip to return from checking their trot lines or from spearfishing.

Flies were a big problem. Shirley hung strips of sticky tape over the table so they could eat in relative peace. One night after the table had been cleared, while the family lingered and talked with dark eyes watching, Larry put Gregory up on the table. As the chubby little fellow careened gleefully down its length, the fly-filled tape strips stuck in his hair. The family laughed and laughed as Shirley tried to rescue him.

Shirley became the village doctor—at least Larry called her Doctor. Dr. Dresser helped by radio and TEAM Irian had a couple of nurses who sometimes flew in to advise. Often it took Larry's muscle to give shots.

For the first time, the Nafaripi at Sumapero had some defenses against malaria, dysentery, pneumonia, and ulcerated wounds and sores, and they were grateful. They brought gifts of food in appreciation for medicines or treatment.

They also had some relief from pain. They were used to burning the cheek to take the mind off a toothache, slitting the forehead to let headache pain bleed out, or rubbing the skin with an itch-causing plant to distract from arthritic pain.

Shirley had two rules. One was that a patient must go down to the river and bathe before appearing at the clinic. One thing the bathing accomplished was to help arrest a scaly skin disease appearing in ugly raised spirals on nearly all of them—a sort of ringworm.

The other rule was that if a patient neglected a course of medication and returned to the clinic, Shirley refused treatment—even to Chief Esapa, as his clan looked on in disbelief. It was the best way she could think of to teach them to consistently take their medicine. This was crucial because if one had dysentery, for example, and didn't complete the prescribed course of sulpha drugs, the disease came right back.

The Rascher children were nonchalant about the nakedness of their neighbors. The Nafaripi considered themselves clothed in a G-string or grass pantie. And the children accepted these things as being their clothes. That was just the way it was. Most of the men began wearing pants soon after the Raschers arrived.

But there was one man who was big and surly, bald and one-eyed and very ugly. When he was very sick he came to Shirley at the clinic stripped of his shorts and laid there in his misery. Even to the other patients waiting at the clinic, this man was naked. He was one of three or four villagers who chose to go fishing instead of attending church—until Shirley successfully treated him for malaria.

Shirley didn't mind raising baby Greg and then Karen, too, in the swamps. She was a good, watchful mother. The children were adaptable and she could care for them about as well in one place as another.

Their childhood illnesses were treated with Dr. Dresser's assistance by radio. Any medications they needed were usually stocked in their own clinic.

Shirley also didn't mind the tediousness of her chores. And she made do without complaint. Had she not chosen this life? Had she not been chosen for it? When the MAF planes were down and their food supplies were running terribly low, she used whatever the natives provided for them. She used sago for pancakes, and in many other ingenious ways, so it wouldn't taste so much like paper. Shirley's attitudes were not lost on daughter Kathy.

Larry had been preaching with his language helper as an interpreter for a year or so, and he had picked up some Nafaripi. He felt he was getting through to them and decided to give an invitation.

At the conclusion of his message one Sunday he invited anyone to come forward if they wanted to invite Jesus Christ into their lives.

Apart from the village dogs and the babies, there was silence. The Nafaripi looked at him quizzically from their logs.

Larry repeated what he'd said, explaining.

Again there was no response. Larry was surprised.

Finally Esapa rose in the back left-hand corner of the room. "*Tuan*, what are you saying to us? Do you mean you want us to come to the front of the church?"

"Yes, if you want to ask Jesus into your life . . ." Larry began.

"*Boppa*, don't you remember that day in the man's house when we all crossed the room to say we wanted to learn about God?"

Unlike in some cultures, a decision of the will, which was made collectively, was not as difficult for the Nafaripi as understanding what the decision would mean in their daily lives.

Larry held baptismal classes and the whole village

wanted to attend. But they were mad as hornets if they didn't pass the course.

One part of life in Sumapero was difficult, particularly for Shirley who was not out with the people as much as Larry. Here at the end of the earth they were terribly, sometimes profoundly, alone, especially when the older children were at school in Sentani. There was noise and activity and chanting to the drums. But there was precious little companionship with "their own kind."

But in their isolation they were also more keenly aware of the presence and protection of their God. When they shared this Psalm in a prayer letter home in 1969, it was because they had found in all respects in their lives it held true.

> *I will lift up my eyes to the mountains;*
> *From whence shall my help come?*
> *My help comes from the Lord,*
> *Who made heaven and earth.*
> *He will not allow your foot to slip;*
> *He who keeps you will not slumber.*
> *Behold, He who keeps Israel*
> *Will neither slumber nor sleep.*
>
> *The Lord is your keeper;*
> *The Lord is your shade on your right hand.*
> *The sun will not smite you by day,*
> *Nor the moon by night.*
> *The Lord will protect you from all evil;*
> *He will keep your soul.*
> *The Lord will guard your going out and your*
> *coming in*
> *From this time forth and forever.*
>
> *Psalm 121, NAS*

The family spent the Christmas of 1969 in Kokonao, as did Moses, who had gone on from Sumapero to begin a school and church among other Nafaripi at the village of Wapu. Jonas, a Bible school graduate and government-approved teacher, had replaced Moses and Benoni in the Sumapero school.

Jonas was a slight fellow, a Biaker and single. He had come to teach at Sumapero mostly because he needed a job. He was congenial and good company, so Larry and Shirley began inviting him to their home for dinner and for game nights on Fridays. He enjoyed little Greg and became like family.

The people of Sumapero went upriver to hunt at Christmas time. The Wapu people, traditional enemies who lived an hour upriver by canoe, surrounded them and threatened war. They shot arrows at them but the clans of Sumapero did not return fire. "We have given up the old ways. We don't want to have war," they said.

When the Raschers returned from Kokonao, Larry was told little of the situation, and had not given what he heard much credence. Rumors were as thick in the swamps as monkey chatter. War rumors were usually started over a supposed love triangle or a stolen pig. Sometimes they perpetuated feuds which had endured for generations. Occasionally these led to kidnapping, revenge, warfare.

Now the men of Wumani clan, helping Larry unload lumber at the river, told him it was beyond rumor. The people of Wapu were making arrows. If Sumapero did not make arrows they would be without defense. If they did make arrows, and word of it reached Wapu, there would certainly be war.

"We must make arrows," said one young Nafaripi. "We are not women. We must defend ourselves."

"These people have forgotten that we know how to kill and eat people," said Esapa when he heard of it, scowling.

"Make some arrows for defense," Larry told them. "If they attack you, I will call for help over the radio. We will pray as a village that the Lord will take from the hearts of Wapu the desire for war."

In a short time the people of Wapu did indeed relinquish the idea and settle back into the adjustments of their own new life in their own new village with Moses' school and church.

Larry bought the arrows which had been made in Sumapero. He later took them to the U.S., for souvenirs of West Irian, and also so that Wapu would not hear of arrows in Sumapero.

After eight months the Rascher's *atap* house was leaning. Larry set to work building the only home which would be the Raschers' very own in West Irian. Its frame and floor and stilts were of ironwood. It had *gaba gaba* walls for insulation from the heat. It had screens on the doors and windows and a corrugated aluminum roof. There were three bedrooms, a living room, dining room, study, bathroom and kitchen: a beautiful home for the middle of a tropical swamp. In addition it had a most handy *gudang* with a wide porch and steps and a window which folded down to form a counter. Here Shirley held clinic, with medical supplies stored along one wall of the *gudang*. Here Larry held his *toko*, selling fish hooks, implements and clothing to the natives. The family stored their barrels of extra clothing and food supplies along the third wall.

When Shirley did have company she did it up right, even when the visit was brief. When Dr. Dresser came to Sumapero to pull teeth, it was usually on a tight schedule of rounds to many villages on the MAF float plane. As the pilot waited, the doctor lined up his patients in the Raschers' yard. On his first pass through he'd ask each one where it hurt. That's where he'd shoot them with Novocain, then send them to the back of the line. By the time each cycled back to him, the drug had taken effect and Doc Dresser could pull teeth. Shirley fixed a nice noonday dinner for him and for MAF Pilot Bob Breuker. She set the table with her best dishes and glasses, with napkins over the glasses to keep flies out of the iced tea. They ate at the table she had asked Larry to build large enough to seat their family and the TEAM Irian field council. The whole process, including dinner, was completed in less than an hour.

Government officials came now and then to inspect the village and the school. During the Raschers' first spring in Sumapero, TEAM Irian's field council of five TEAM missionaries met at Sumapero to see its newest mission station. Larry and Shirley were proud to show their guests around.

When Larry was off hauling lumber on a building project with colleague Chuck Preston, Bernita and the Preston kids came for a visit. While the children played, the women took full advantage of the rare opportunity to talk with an understanding woman friend.

By the summer of 1970, more than fifty Nafaripi believers in Jesus Christ had been baptized in the Cemara River. The school was thriving. Jonas was capably teaching the school and helping the Nafaripi leadership in the church. New believers were eager to learn all they could about God. The Christian Nafaripi had decided they should not take more wives than they already had. Quarrel and rumor were waning in the village. The work of felling trees had begun for the construction of an airstrip. Little Gregory and now Karen were growing up speaking Indonesian with the village children.

The Raschers were due for their furlough year in the U.S. Larry and Shirley, although happy in the village, were both thin and exhausted. They longed to see family and friends in the States. Reluctantly, they said goodbye to the Nafaripi, who sang to the drums throughout the night before the Raschers left, composing story-songs about them which are perhaps still sung sometimes, somewhere. Keith and Chip, home from school and packed up for the States, got up now and then through the night to keep the chanters company.

With TEAM Irian short-handed as usual, the station was to be checked on, but basically unmanned by missionaries until the Raschers returned.

Jonas had said he would not stay in Sumapero without Larry and Shirley, but he did stay. He stayed with little pay, eating native food, with no friends except primitive Nafaripi, whose language he was still learning, taking few vacations. He helped the Nafaripi build a new church, taking pride in placing every stalk himself in the *gaba gaba* ceiling. He stayed without grumbling week after week, year after year, and eventually paid for his faithfulness.

FURLOUGH

A summer day in St. Louis didn't feel much different than any day in Sumapero, except that Larry's father and step-mother Edna had an attic fan. The Rascher family lived with Larry's folks, visited with Shirley's mother, and generally enjoyed summer in America. Kathy, Keith and Chip felt at home at Grandma and Grandpa's house and settled right in. Greg was surprised to discover Grandpa was not a tape recorder, because he had only heard Grandpa's voice on tape.

Karen at a year old wanted to get accustomed to this new world with a firm grasp on her mommy or daddy. Edna tried everything she could think of to win Karen's confidence. She held her in the yard one day while Shirley was busy in the house. She was amazed that Karen let her. Reaching up, Edna helped Karen pluck a leaf from a tree. Edna twirled it in her fingers, tickling Karen's nose. Karen laughed and laughed, with a child's laugh which is complete abandon and utterly infectious. Edna picked another leaf and helped Karen twirl it in her tiny fingers close to Edna's nose. They both laughed till Edna could hardly hold her. Chip came out the back door and walked over to see what he was missing. "You've got it made, Grandma," he said.

Before school started, the family settled in Michigan, and real life began. The five churches which contributed the majority of the Raschers' support were within fifty miles of one another in southwestern Michigan. Each furlough they lived in one of these towns: Spring Lake, Zeeland, Wyoming Park, Hudsonville, or Holland. Larry could travel to any of the churches to preach or attend meetings and be home the same day. The churches thereabouts thought Larry a good preacher, and getting better. He didn't preach on a book he'd read or on what he'd heard other people say. He shared what the Lord had told him through the Bible and through his experiences. Each of the churches had a women's missionary society to which Shirley spoke. The family was spared the constant travel to supporting churches that can be wearing on a missionary family.

This time they rented a house in Wyoming Park. The Wyoming Park Baptist Church took good care of its missionaries at home. It's people brought the Raschers produce from their gardens and helped supply the family with winter clothes. Whenever anyone in the family had a birthday, two families, the Breukers and Bosmas, brought over a birthday cake. Each Saturday morning a lady from Hudsonville showed up to give Shirley a complimentary shampoo and set.

Larry worked for a builder when he wasn't occupied at one of the five churches. He told story after story on the job. After listening to Larry, and sensing a call himself, Jim Bruursema eventually took his wife and children to West Irian to build for the Lord there.

This was the first time the seven Raschers had lived an entire year together, and they loved it. Greg and Karen were the family's centerpieces. Their antics were enjoyed fivefold.

Karen had a rubber ducky which she brought in to show Shirley one day. It had been scribbled over by Greg with a pen. "Mommy, Greg in trouble!" Karen said solemnly. It was her first sentence.

They lived on a cul-de-sac in a neighborhood that housed a friend for each Rascher child. They taught the neighbor kids Irianese games—or at least games they played in West Irian like "Capture the Flag." The neighborhood kids waited impatiently through Rascher mealtimes till the kids could come out and play. In turn, neighborhood friends taught them to play football, baseball and basketball.

Keith and Chip tore around on a mini-bike. They helped Greg build forts in the basement. They watched *Gilligan's Island, Gunsmoke,* and *Bonanza* on TV.

The kids adjusted well to school in Michigan. Academically they always came back to the States with a bit of an edge, which helped. In the public schools they attended their teachers were often Christians, or at the least they empathized with the children in their year of changes. Chip was in the fifth grade and Kathy and Keith were in the eighth.

Keith discovered that the other kids thought it was pretty neat that he could speak another language. They asked him how to say various things in Indonesian. He could entertain an audience, too, with tales of eating bats and grubs and cassowary birds. He didn't quite understand the dating that went on between eighth grade boys and girls because the kids in Sentani weren't doing that. He turned down an offer of $10 if he would cuss. The offer caught him by surprise because Keith didn't think of himself as different from the other kids. Keith loved Irian and he missed it. But basically Keith didn't care where they lived; he wanted to have fun.

After sweltering day on end for four years, the Rascher kids were up for all the snow a Michigan winter could deliver. They built snow forts and snowmen and made snow angels, tried skiing on a small run, and of course went sledding. Chip tried a saucer his first time out. They tramped up the sledding hill, a good steep one in Wyoming Park. "Now Chip, hold on no matter what," Larry instructed. Chip did— even when the saucer hit a tree stump and sailed through the air.

Larry had a little detective work to do that furlough. It was part of a grand scheme he had hatched for the people of Sumapero. It was about peanut butter.

Larry knew a missionary in the interior of West Irian whose tribe grew peanuts. The missionary sent them to the coast where they were processed with a small hand grinder. He then sent peanut butter to each missionary family on the island.

The Nafaripi needed protein in their diet, and they needed a cash crop. Peanuts would grow in salt water if planted on fairly high ground. Larry decided the people of Sumapero could produce peanuts for all of West Irian.

Larry had lain awake nights in Irian refining his plan. Now he found an old-fashioned peanut butter factory in Wyoming Park, Michigan. Larry explained his idea at the factory. Did they know where he could find a large grinder?

"Sure. We've got an old one in the back we'll sell you for $200." It had been built at the turn of the century and wasn't exactly portable. It must have weighed 500 pounds. But it suited Larry fine.

Its electric motor would be of no use in West Irian, so a friend helped Larry rig up a ten horsepower Kohler engine with a pulley system to run the grinder. They disassembled the grinder carefully, drawing diagrams of how the parts fit together, so he could ship it to the mission field.

The friend sent Larry to a restaurant in Grand Rapids where he had located a commercial roaster: a huge tub holding four stainless steel baskets with long handles. The Nafaripi could roast their peanuts in coconut oil. He grew impatient to get back to the field with his equipment and ideas.

Larry wedged in a course in linguistics at Grand Rapids School of Bible and Missions. He and Shirley tried to make headway with their reams of Nafaripi language notes.

Shirley came down with malaria during Larry's school term—the only time she was to have it, but it was severe. Her head swelled like a pumpkin and was scorching hot. Kathy took charge of Gregory and Karen as much as she could, and fellow students from Larry's class brought in meals.

Kathy worked hard to help and was frightened to see her mother this way. It was a great relief to her when the fever subsided.

By spring the family had a sufficiency of snow and crisp weather, and the joys of having family and good friends nearby. They had done all the things they had said "We're going to get to do. . ." on furlough—or they had decided they weren't worth doing after all. They were all healthy and a few pounds heavier. The drums and the chants of Sumapero, their home, were calling them.

For the last women's group Shirley addressed, she began by quoting a houseboy they had taken from Sumapero to work for them during a stint back in Kokonao: "I like your food. I like your people. I like your home. But I want to go home." Shirley felt this way too, and could say goodbye without many tears. She wrote this to friends: "Lawrence has just completed the first house we could call 'our own.' It is the nicest home anyone could wish to have on a primitive mission station, a split level, furnished with nice furniture, some of which is made by my carpenter husband, and a lot of which were gifts from many praying friends. I love and enjoy it, but it's not something that I couldn't leave if the Lord should direct to another place. He continues to meet every need, every day in every place."

It was not that they looked to utopia, but a work ordained to be their work, a home that was their home. "Do you think you'll be able to settle back in easily?" a friend asked Shirley.

"I don't know," Shirley thought about it. "Sometimes missionaries have something traumatic happen when they return to the field—almost as a sort of testing."

Folks from Wyoming Park Baptist Church helped them pack and clean the house. Packing for four or five years of a family of seven's personal, household and work needs was a staggering task. Within their twenty drums and crates were a new set of Melamec dishes from the church in Spring Lake; lots of records; power tools including a new electric chain saw; a new camera with telephoto lens; gifts for the children for Christmases and birthdays, including a toy piano for Greg and Karen; a new Maytag washing machine; medical supplies; clothing for all; a clarinet and saxophone; a peanut grinder and roaster; and a new rocking chair. Each of these provisions was a reminder of the many friends and the churches who were faithful in support of the Raschers with gifts and with prayers—and of God's provision in the lives of these people.

People like D. J. DePree, founder of the Herman Miller Furniture Company in Zeeland, Michigan. Everyone in Zeeland knew Mr. DePree. He was a wealthy man. He was also a man whose every move was committed to the Lord. He had started the church in Ventura, just north of Holland, where Larry had interned as pastor and had been ordained.

At the close of the Rascher's earlier furlough in 1966, Mr. DePree had arranged to have Larry and Shirley meet him at Van Raalte's Restaurant in Zeeland. At Van Raalte's the waitresses knew Mr. DePree's standing order. He had an imposing countenance, with a large, hooked nose and long, bushy eyebrows. He sat opposite Larry and Shirley with a note pad and pencil. He had just that week seen the Raschers' slides on the work in West Irian.

"Is it safe for you to travel to these villages with your family in a dugout canoe?" he asked.

"Well, not really, but that's all we have," Larry replied, amused at his businesslike friend with the big heart.

"What would it take to be safe?"

"A boat."

"What kind?"

"Aluminum would be better than fiberglass because of the logs in the rivers," said Larry.

"And what motor?"

"A forty or sixty horsepower Johnson would be about right."

"And what about these natives?" Mr. DePree asked. "What would help them?"

"I'd like to be able to take some big fish nets for them. . . and a generator to use for power tools. The Hudsonville church bought a large generator, but we use it for the school."

"About what would this, this, and this cost?" asked Mr. DePree, pointing to the items on his pad and figuring the answer to his own question. I'll send a check to TEAM for these items. You go to Hudsonville Marine on Highway 21 and find a boat big enough."

As usual there was no fanfare. "You don't need to tell anyone," said D.J. "You need it." The meal and the meeting were completed. Mr. DePree was soon on his way back to the office, leaving the couple stunned but excited.

They took their family farewells in St. Louis. The hardest was Shirley's mother, who was hospitalized from a heart attack. She regularly had a heart attack around the time Larry and Shirley left for the field. Shirley battled guilt over her mother's health. But she also had overwhelming peace that West Irian was where her mother really wanted them to be, hard as it was for her.

An exception was made in the hospital rules to allow Karen and Greg into their grandmother's room. They sat on the foot of her bed and sang "Jesus Loves Me" for her, two fresh little cherubs, as both mother and grandmother watched tearfully.

This time the walk back down the hospital corridor in early summer of 1971 really was goodbye. Grandma Ray would go to be with her Lord after her ninth heart attack in 1973. But before that Shirley would be saying a harder goodbye.

JOURNEY TO KOKONAO

On the morning of July 24, 1971, the Ebenezer, Larry's new boat, gently swayed at anchor in the mouth of the Koperapoka River. It was their first preaching trip to Kokonao after furlough in Michigan. Keith and Kathy had flown to Faith Academy in Manila. Moses was aboard with the rest of them. It was fun to be out on the boat together, back at work.

Perhaps four hours of their journey remained. They would head ten miles out to sea to get past the mud flats to deeper water, then follow the shoreline to the mouth of the Tipuka River. It was not far up the Tipuka to Kokonao.

Chip had been up late the night before and was asleep in the cabin for the first hour out to sea. Shirley read to Karen and Gregory under the canopy: Greg's favorite book *Dear Little Deer* and a Bible story book. As the sea grew choppier, Gregory suggested "Let's ask God to help us now." Chip woke up and helped Shirley get the little ones into the cabin. Moses brought in radios, cameras, and other gear they didn't want to get wet.

By 8:00 a.m. the rain began, and behind it came a tremendous east wind. Chip was excited to encounter waves after two monotonous days on the river. He had been in waves before with Larry, and it was fun. Chip climbed out of the cabin and yelled to Larry, steering from the roof. "How bad is it, Dad?"

"It's bad, but nothing to worry about." Chip knew, though, that it was something to worry about as he watched his dad fight to keep the boat steady.

Larry struggled to keep the boat cutting the waves head on. Between swells he tried to turn the boat around and go back, but they were traveling against the waves back to the east and with them to the west. He resumed his course. The swells were still manageable and he hoped to get to the buoys of the Tipuka River mouth before they got worse.

The waves rose steadily, pounding the boat. Larry tried to turn in toward the river that came before the Tipuka, but the river mouth was shallow and the breakers were higher in the shallow water. As they got near the river mouth, the boat tossed like a carnival ride.

Again Larry turned the boat and its precious cargo out to sea. His heart was calling out to God to save them. Why had he come this way? What should he do?

They were taking on water. Shirley and Moses bailed frantically. Chip held Karen and Greg in the cabin. All three children were frightened and seasick.

Larry had to go far out to sea to get around the long Tipuka sandbar. By now the waves crested at fifteen to twenty feet. Green walls of water crashed against the Ebenezer. Larry headed into the biggest ones, then northwest toward shore in between them. When he tried to point toward shore, waves slammed the boat from the back, nearly flipping it end over end.

Heading toward land was futile, so again Larry turned toward open sea, praying that as the tide went out the sea would subside. The Ebenezer and Larry fought valiantly, but the waves were coming from all directions rather than in rows. He glanced back to see two waves collide at the stern of the boat and lay a wall of water into it. The engine gurgled sickeningly. The Ebenezer was dead in the water.

The boat began to fill. Shirley was astonished. She had never considered the possibility that the boat would not make it to the river mouth. Still, she didn't panic. She handed Karen and Greg through the hole in the cabin roof to Larry. Shirley climbed out after them. Chip pulled on the cabin door, which stuck in its wooden track. Frantically he pulled and pulled until it finally slid open, and he got out. The boat filled, rolled on its side, then turned completely over while they thrashed around in the chilly sea.

Shirley could tell that Chip was very frightened. "Chipper," she yelled to him above the tumult, "the Lord knows where we are and everything about the situation." From then on Chip was composed, helpful, and no longer afraid.

All six of them tried to climb onto the bottom of the boat from the same side, causing it to spin. Moses held Karen; Larry held Greg. They spread out around the bottom of the boat to hold onto it. Shirley's watch had stopped. It was 10:20 a.m. There was no sign of human life anywhere. They could barely see the shore.

They were able to float with the boat, bracing for each oncoming wave. A two-inch keel stuck up from the center of the bottom. They each grasped it and worked their way up the keel to the bow, huddling together there to anticipate the next wave. The waves slammed them to the back of the boat. If anyone lost hold of the keel, sliding back, he could grab the propeller guard at the stern. But if they stayed at the stern the boat would spin, so between waves they had to work their way up the keel again. It was particularly hard for Larry and Moses, who could only grab hold with one arm. They made progress slowly toward shore, but as they got closer the breakers rose.

The men cradled the children against their chests as waves broke over their backs. They helped Karen and Greg to hold their noses, but the children were taking in water, coughing and sputtering. Greg said to Larry, "I like swimmin', Daddy, but I'm ready to go home now and get some milk." They were shivering.

At about noon the anchor lodged in sand on the bottom. They could no longer move toward shore and the boat rolled with each wave. They had nothing sharp enough to cut the rope. No one spoke, as it took all their energy to anticipate each wave and hang onto the gyrating boat. By now Karen's big eyes were glassy, and she sat slumped over on Moses' shoulders. Still, when Shirley smiled at her, Karen managed a weak smile back.

Chip's senses were still keen and he was able to do many things that Moses and Larry couldn't, as they were struggling to hold the children, and that Shirley couldn't, because of exhaustion.

Chip had an idea. He slowly worked his way to the front of the boat. He had noticed that the largest of the swells momentarily freed the anchor. When a big one came he dove down twenty, thirty, forty feet along the anchor rope. On his second try he pulled the anchor to the surface with him and tied it to the front of the boat. Again the wreck inched inland.

By afternoon Larry's arm was near breaking with the weight of his sturdy, water-logged little boy. A mighty surge wrenched Greg from Larry's grasp and flung him fifty feet from the boat. Larry swam frantically for the boy, but by the time he got to him Greg was floating face-down in the water. Larry swam to the boat with the bloated little body. Miserably, Larry tried and tried to tie Greg's body to the boat. But he couldn't bring himself to tie the body tightly enough, and the waves kept loosening it.

"Lawrence, let him go. That's not Greg," said Shirley. By God's grace they were becoming able to divorce this flesh from the being of their dear son. Moses called that he could no longer hold Karen, so Larry took her tiny, limp body.

"Shirley, I'm sorry," cried Larry in agony. Shirley reached for his hand on the keel.

Shirley was weakened by the ordeal and was the next one propelled away. A weak swimmer at best, there was no reason Shirley should survive. But she rolled over and floated on her back. Larry and Moses pulled her back to the boat.

For the week prior to the trip Shirley had been caught by a longing in her heart to see the Lord. Perhaps they all would today. She was glad for Keith and Kathy's sake that the Logans, their legal guardians, had made a special trip from Michigan to see them off at the St. Louis airport.

At about 3:00 p.m. the Ebenezer grounded on a sandbar in fifteen feet of water. Waves smashed the boat apart, and Karen, too, was thrown from Larry's arm. They searched frantically but never saw Karen's body again. By now none of them expected to live, so keeping bodies didn't seem to matter. "Mom and Dad, if we don't make it," said Chip, "we're all Christians." It was heartrending to see their children so trusting and brave.

Moses was watching Larry and Shirley. He had not seen among the natives any parents who loved their children more than these *tuans* did. If they wailed and grieved now surely all of them would be lost. But Moses had never before seen such resignation. *The Lord gives and the Lord takes away.* He had not seen such peace.

When the boat smashed to pieces, the plywood canopy remained intact. Shirley was on top of the canopy when the boat splintered. Chip and Moses were thrown twenty-five yards away. "Dad, should we come back to you and Mom?" Chip yelled. There was no longer a boat for them to cling to.

"Chip, you and Moses swim for shore. I'll stay with Mom." They were still about three miles out.

If Larry got on the canopy with Shirley it sank. For a while he trod water holding onto it, too spent to do more. Eventually he swam, pushing the canopy with Shirley on it. The plank partly submerged under Shirley's weight so that her head was just above water. Chip looked back once to see his parents' heads bobbing along together. Larry kicked until near dark, heading toward the island. The breakers were small but choppy and constant as they got closer in. He and Shirley were battered, weary and cold.

The channel of a river ran along the ocean side of the island. As they got closer to shore the current carried them back out to sea. "Shirley, we're not going to be any closer. We're going back out to sea. Do you think you could swim?" Larry asked.

Shirley could barely speak or move. "No. There's no hope for me to swim ten feet." So that was that. Larry would not leave her and they just floated and hung on. They didn't know whether Chip and Moses would make it. Their friends the Logans in Michigan would be good guardians for Keith and Kathy, and for Chip if he survived.

Larry had had the physical strength to bring them this far, but he did not think of himself as the stronger one. His heart was like putty. Curiously, from within Shirley's soul now came swells of praise, of verses and hymns tucked there years ago, of bits of Bible study lessons from Wyoming Park. *"My priorities in God's eyes are first, Himself and second, my husband,"* she thought. *"And my husband is still here and needs me."*

"I keep thinking of a song from freshman choir," Shirley murmured. "The billows are high, but the Lord is above them and mighty." Both were keenly conscious of the presence of God with them. As they floated they praised God—though their bodies were spent and their minds were dazed with their loss.

Larry let go. He slid off the canopy and underwater.

His foot hit a fallen tree about eight feet down. He pushed back up to the surface with a burst of strength. They were not in deep water. The island had a long sandbar. The tide was going out.

Larry took Shirley's arm and persuaded her to leave the canopy. They jumped toward shore, submerging and then springing off the bottom: down, up and forward. They gulped air when their heads broke the surface.

Night came as they stumbled up the beach. They fell on their knees and thanked the Lord for firm ground, for the Presence they felt, for their lives—for the opportunity to at least raise Kathy and Keith. They prayed: "Lord, help us to love little children like never before."

It was dark, moonless. The millions of stars lowered the ceiling of heaven. They did not feel alone, though it was windy and cold in their shredded clothing after hours in the sea.

Larry tried to bury Shirley in the sand to warm her, but the sand was alive with creatures, and she found herself growing stiff unless she moved.

They snuggled together and quietly talked and prayed. Shirley knew that Larry was carrying the whole burden of their ordeal. She was flooded with a love for him greater than she had ever experienced.

The tide was far out. Larry reasoned that they could start now and hope to walk to the mainland. If they waited for morning, they'd have to swim to it. As they walked Shirley told Larry that the Lord was giving her an overwhelming desire to be more of a helpmeet to him than ever before. They shared precious words and audibly praised their God.

They called out for Moses and Chip, but heard only the waves and the wind in the palms. They could not split up to search for them, nor had they energy to do so. They clung to each other as if they were one person, a larger one who had survived an experience of awesome magnitude.

After a few hours of rest, they stumbled on in the darkness through the mud toward land. There was no sense even worrying about what they might be stepping on. They could see nothing.

A stream ran midway between the island and mainland. They got to its channel and were relieved to find the water only waist deep and the bottom fairly firm.

They collapsed on the far bank, panting and shivering. "Let's go, Shirley." Larry took her elbow and helped her up. "We're almost there."

But on this final stretch the mud was like quicksand and they couldn't unstick themselves from it and move forward.

Shirley was singing haltingly, between breathes, but the sound was amazingly loud and firm in the night: "I will sing to the Lord as long as I live: I will sing praise to my God while I have my being."

"Shirley, don't waste your energy singing!" Larry chided.

"I can't help it. So many verses He's giving me."

They reached the point where neither could resist the mire enough to move. Larry's fingers touched a branch. There were two or three of them, each about four feet long.

They sat in the mud and tried to use the wood like snowshoes to help them scootch backwards. With sticks in each hand, Larry placed the sticks in the mud as far in back of him as he could reach. He pulled himself backward to the wood. Shirley held onto his foot with both hands and pulled herself up to his foot. They made a little progress, but they couldn't keep this up long.

"Shirley, we've got to change course."

"Yes, we've got to try something."

"If we head west, parallel to the shore, I know there's a beach and higher ground that way."

Just before dawn they found the beach. The ground

was firmer, but pocked with deep crevices. They kept falling. Sometimes one caught the other; sometimes one pulled the other down.

"What's that?" At daylight Shirley thought she heard voices. They called back. Their mouths were so dry that the sound was parched and thin. The breeze bore no answer. They lay in shallow water to wash off the mud, which pulled at their sunburned skin as it caked. They rinsed out their mouths with salt water.

Where the tree line began they spotted an abandoned native bivouac, a few cut branches bound and shaped with rattan vines and covered with leaf matting. Natives built these as temporary camp sites where they were hunting sago. The shelter measured about eight feet by six feet. Larry and Shirley huddled in it and prayed for direction.

When Larry opened his eyes from praying he saw at his feet the bottom of a rotting canoe. It was shaped like a surfboard. It must have been used as a walkway from the bivouac.

If they were to get help, Larry would have to swim across a river, walk several miles through the jungle and cross a second wide river to the mining company. He saw this as the Lord's provision: a kickboard, a floating board, for the first river. It gave him assurance that he should leave Shirley in the bivouac and go on.

Halfway around the world in Lake Orion, Michigan, a pastor's wife, a friend, had awakened in the middle of the night burdened to pray for Larry and Shirley. She continued in prayer for them until dawn.

It was nearly noon when Moses and Chip began their swim in the pitching surf. Moses was the more worried of the two. He had never swum nearly so far in rough water. Then there was the boy. . . . He felt responsible for Chip, and he was scared.

There was also the matter of a deep gash in his left foot, which was bleeding badly. He had not mentioned it to any of the others. They had enough to deal with, but what if it drew sharks or crocs? Not only to him, but to the boy? Moses had one sock left on. He worked it off his right foot in the waves and put it on his left, over the cut. He was exhausted from fighting the waves with the little girl. Moses prayed for strength. *"If you spare me, Lord, I will serve you always."*

For a while Moses tried to swim alongside Chip. At school in Sentani, Chip had learned to swim a strong crawl stroke. But Moses was a strong man and a much faster swimmer. It was hard on Moses to tread water and wait for him. Chip told him to go on.

Chip wasn't afraid. He felt little of anything. He just told himself over and over to keep swimming. He was no longer at war with the waves, as he had been around the wrecked boat. Now the swells propelled him toward shore. For hours he swam in the cold green sea. *Keep swimming.* He swam toward two points of land, watching to see which would prove closer. A couple of times he saw Moses far ahead of him on the crest of a wave. But by mid-afternoon he saw him no more. *Stroke. Stroke.* Chip's arms felt like lead, but he forced them to arch, then pull.

The sun set. By this time he had determined that the point of land to the left was an island and was closer. He could see its dark bulk in the dusk, and he swam.

He heard a sound, a cry—his first sound other than the splashing and the pounding for hours. His eyes searched the shore. The dark shape of Moses was high in a palm tree calling to him. "Stand up! Stand up!"

Chip straightened his arms and touched bottom with his fingertips. He was swimming in two feet of water.

Chip knew from his storybooks that this was where he would stagger onto the beach, fall down exhausted and sleep for two days. He waded in, shivering violently as the wind whipped his body, naked except for his underwear.

Moses helped Chip into the trees where there was some shelter from the wind and where he had piled some clams. They could do nothing but lie shaking for a long while. Moses tried to build a fire but hadn't the strength to pull the ratan chord back and forth. Toward sunset they sought better shelter for the night.

Moses found a hollow place beneath the roots of a fallen tree where they would be sheltered from the wind. He scattered pine needles under them. Chip was still trembling and sore. They slept fitfully. "If Mom and Dad don't make it, I'll have to go back to the States," said Chip. "I've just been there and I don't want to go back. I want to stay here." He could hear the surf but could not see it in the darkness. There was no moon.

"The Lord spared both of us for something, Chip. I know I am not strong enough to swim that far, and you are just a boy. I know He will take care of you. He knows what is best. Try to sleep. In the morning we will pray about what we should do."

In the morning it felt strange to Chip to get up and move on without any camping gear to pack. Debris from the Ebenezer was strewn along the beach, and they scavenged for food. They were both timid in their search. What if they found bodies? Yet if there were bodies, particularly Larry's or Shirley's, they needed to find them. They found a Tupperware container, a doll of Karen's, a cabbage, a papaya—bits of home life torn in pieces. Chip insisted they save half the cabbage and half the papaya for his mom and dad.

Also littering the beach that morning were some old fifty-five-gallon drums, probably from the mining company. They talked of lashing the drums together to make a raft which would take them from the island to shore. But they decided they needed to pray about what they should do. If Larry and Shirley were on the island or the shore, how would they find one another? They both had a strong sense that there was a right and a wrong way to go.

Each of them prayed simply, thanking the Lord for their lives, asking for help in finding Larry and Shirley.

As they finished and looked out over the ocean a white bird swooped past them heading west. Soon it reappeared. Three times the bird circled the island. Moses knew that when a bird circled it meant humans were present. He told Chip he believed his folks were alive, and also on the island. The two walked along the beach toward the west as the bird had, even though they knew this way led to the ocean side of the island, not the mainland side.

As they walked they picked through cargo from the boat: the movie camera, the short wave radio, the address book with all the entries washed away, clothing.

At the western end of the island they could see both a beach and the mainland in the distance to the west. Directly between them and the shore stretched two miles of mud flats. The tide was still low enough that they could walk most of the way to the beach.

When they reached land they walked some distance apart to check through the debris. Chip spotted footprints and called to Moses. "These belong to your parents, Chip," said Moses. "No native has feet that come up off the ground in the middle."

As the two followed the footprints they could see where the couple had fallen or laid down to rest in the sand; most often where just Shirley fell. Chip worried about his mom. They followed the footprints through tangled jungle undergrowth and manggi-manggi roots like bleached, arthritic fingers. It was slow, painful going without a machete or shoes or protective clothing.

Mid-morning they found Shirley lying in the bivouac where Larry had left her.

Shirley held her sandy-haired, freckle-faced son, who looked little the worse for this initiation into manhood, and thanked God for sparing their lives. Shirley's eyes were swollen, her face was red and her body a patchwork of bruises. She was too weak to sit up, but she devoured the halves of papaya and cabbage. "Hey, but what about Dad?" Chip protested.

Larry rested across the river from the mining company; help was within sight. He and Shirley would make it. "Lord, I don't have strength to swim across. But I hope I'm far enough up river that I can float across with the current." Larry entered the brown water, lay on his back and watched the treetops as he floated backward. He consciously relaxed his neck. His screaming leg muscles slowly loosened. Playing through his mind was a chorus he had stroked to across the first river, swimming on his surfboard: *I will sing of the mercies of the Lord forever; I will sing, I will sing.* He let the current carry him as it wished. It took him to the other side.

Mimika families were camped near where Larry crawled out of the river. He knew some of them from Kokonao, but they didn't recognize him, covered with mud. The clothing left on him was in shreds.

"*Swanggi, swanggi!*" they shrieked as they saw him: "evil spirit rising from the water!" They fled into the foliage. He crawled, crying for help in Indonesian. No one would come near him until he caught the eye of a boy, Timotius, from the church in Kokonao.

"Timotius! It's *Bapak Pendita* Rascher." The boy hesitated, then came running. The others followed. They half-carried Larry to the mining company office.

A helicopter was readied for a flight to the mining company hospital up the mountain. Three boats took off immediately to search for Shirley, Chip and Moses.

Larry was given a mug of sweetened hot milk, a favorite Dutch drink that Larry couldn't stand. In this case it was the best thing he had ever put into his mouth.

When the other three were brought by boat, minutes later, to the shore where the helicopter waited, Chip found his dad lying on a stretcher. Somehow it wasn't as much of a shock to see his mom look as she did as it was to see his dad. Chip's father was his hero. He remembered the day he had seen native chiefs at the village of Amar carry Larry through the village on their shoulders, chanting and hollering, because Larry had averted war. Chip gazed now at a man battered and broken trying to save his family. Forever after Chip would be able to comprehend beyond most children how Christ had shed his blood—and died—for Chip Rascher.

ACQUAINTED WITH GRIEF

D ave Hoisington was not sure he was up to the task before him. His fellow MAF Pilot Bob Breuker had contacted him by radio. It was a few days after the Raschers' accident and Bob was flying Larry, Shirley, and Chip to Sentani for a memorial service for Greg and Karen. Chip would stay for school. The Raschers asked to see Dave and his wife Ruth at the airstrip—only them.

Larry and Shirley loved their kids so much. What could Dave say to them? Dave thought of the little scene he and Larry liked to play whenever Dave flew into Kokonao. He wondered what his buddy would be like now.

Dave opened the door of the Cessna 180. Shirley sat next to the pilot; Larry and Chip were on the bench in the back. Larry and Shirley were weeping, and three inches of Kleenex covered the floor of the plane. They were badly bruised and sunburned, and trails of red methiolate crisscrossed their arms and legs. Shirley was dressed almost comically in a native skirt and blouse from the *toko* at the mining company. A little man had given Shirley his shoes.

Dave took them to his home next to the airstrip where Ruth had prepared a meal. Ruth had sent their young children to a neighbor's to play.

"What happened, Larry?" Dave asked his buddy gently as they sat down in the living room. Larry had not thought he wanted to talk about it, but the story rolled out of him like the waves which had kept coming and coming. He continued the story through dinner, repeating over and over, "We were in the water so long." Shirley was very quiet. Chip ate quietly and went out to play.

Ruth took Shirley into their *gudang* and opened the drums of new clothing they'd been saving. She found clothes that would fit Shirley and some for Larry, particularly underwear for both, which they couldn't buy at the mining company *toko*.

The pain was not eased, but Shirley and Larry felt safe and cared for, and they appreciated the kindness. After a rest in the afternoon, Larry went next door to the MAF guest house to tell the story to some of the many missionary friends who had come to Sentani for the memorial service. Several of them noted that Larry seemed more composed than they did.

In the simple ironwood Sentani chapel, Shirley was conscious of the breeze through the screen near her. For the first time in years she had no young children restless beside her. *She had no young children.* Gratitude and sorrow battled inside her, but one thing she knew quite clearly—she knew what she did have. She rehearsed these orderly thoughts above her pain.

She had her relationship to God, whom, though some would have doubted this, Shirley had found to be entirely faithful to her. She had her relationship to her husband, who had never needed her more. She was mother to her surviving children—how she ached to see all three together! Her senses yearned to be made certain that these three were still alive. Their very lives would console her.

Next in importance was her home. Shirley loved to cook and keep up her home. The work was satisfying, and she was good at it. But now she didn't have a

THE RASCHERS,
1961

A VILLAGE IN
KOKONAO

MOSES CARRYING RICE

VILLAGE LIFE IN KOKONAO

RASCHERS' BACKYARD AT HIGH TIDE IN KOKONAO

CHIP AND DR. TJOA

KEITH MOWING
THE LAWN

CHIP, KEITH AND KATHY
RASCHER IN KOKONAO

 LARRY PREPARES NEEDLES DURING CHOLERA EPIDEMIC ON THE SOUTH COAST

ADZING A DUGOUT CANOE

 LARRY BUILDING A HOSPITAL IN PIRIMAPUN, WEST IRIAN

LARRY AND EVERT, PIRIMAPUN HOSPITAL 1963

ASMATERS DANCING AT THE DEDICATION OF THE PIRIMAPUN HOSPITAL

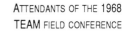
ATTENDANTS OF THE 1968
TEAM FIELD CONFERENCE

KATHY HOLDING GREGORY,
1968

TAUMANAMO, ESAPA'S FIRST
WIFE AND SHIRLEY'S FRIEND

LARRY AND SHIRLEY
WITH JONAS, JOHANA
AND BABY

▲ LARRY AND BENONI BAPTIZE
A BELIEVER AT SUMAPERO

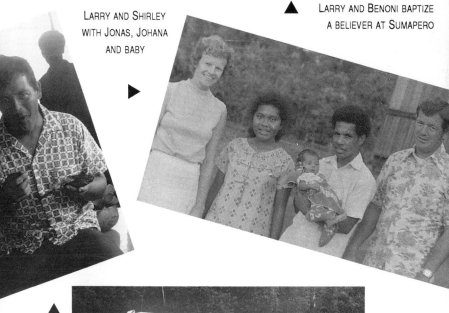

▲
EATING FISH
WHILE HAULING
LUMBER ON THE
MOTOR MOPPI

THE MOTOR
MOPPI METAL
LAUNCH

◀

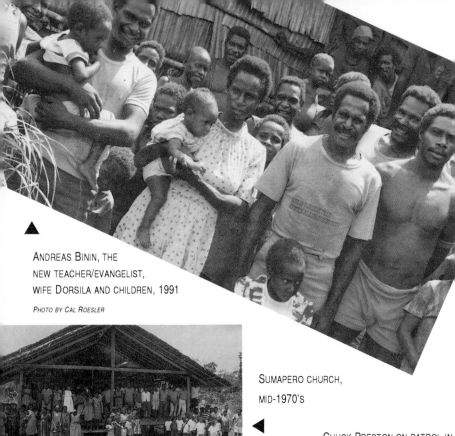

ANDREAS BININ, THE
NEW TEACHER/EVANGELIST,
WIFE DORSILA AND CHILDREN, 1991

PHOTO BY CAL ROESLER

SUMAPERO CHURCH,
MID-1970'S

CHUCK PRESTON ON PATROL IN
MIKE PAPPA LIMA FLOATPLANE

VIEW OF SUMAPERO
FROM RASCHER'S
PORCH, 1973

WOMEN AND CHILDREN OF SUMAPERO (WITH
THE WAITIKO TRIBE MAN'S HOUSE BEHIND), 1970

SUMAPERO CHURCH, 1991
PHOTO BY CAL ROESLER

NAFARIPI OF SUMAPERO, 1972

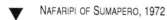

THE SOUTH COAST AT LOW TIDE

◀ GREGORY AND KAREN RASCHER
AT VENTURA BAPTIST CHURCH,
HOLLAND, MICHIGAN

▼ THE HOUSE LARRY BUILT IN SUMAPERO

▲
CONCERT BAND
AT SENTANI
SCHOOL

▶
CHIP, SHIRLEY,
LARRY, KATHY
AND KEITH
AT CHIP'S
9TH GRADE
GRADUATION

CONSTRUCTION ON THE RASCHER
CHILDREN MEMORIAL HOSTEL

MEMORIAL
PLAQUE AT
THE TEAM
HOSTEL IN
SENTANI

MAF PILOT BOB
BRUEKER, 1970

THE REMAINING
RASCHER FAMILY
IN SAOWI

MAF PILOT
DAVE AND RUTH
HOISINGTON
WITH SONS DAN
AND DOUG

THE TEAM BOOKSTORE
IN MANOKWARI

CONSTRUCTION OF THE WOSI
CHURCH, MANOKWARI

FAITH ACADEMY, MANILA

▲ COMPLETED WOSI
CHURCH

▲

ONE OF THE EARLY
CHURCHES ON NUMFOOR

THE MUJIZAT HANGS ANCHOR ▲

◄

LARRY AND CREW
OF MUJIZAT

WOMEN'S QUARTERS ABOARD THE MUJIZAT ▼

▲ The native boat that made the crossing to Numfoor in the storm

Main Street of Bawai

▲ LARRY PREACHING IN
THE BALIEM VALLEY, 1974

KATHY RASCHER AND LORRAINE
LUNOW WITH DANIS
▼

RASCHER'S INDONESIAN BIBLE STUDY,
DENVER, COLORADO, 1987 ▶

SHORT TERM MISSION GROUP, 1985

SHIRLEY WITH WOMEN OF
THE WOSI CHURCH, 1989 ▶

LARRY WITH MEN OF THE WOSI CHURCH, 1989

▲ LARRY'S "TRAVELING WOOD SHED"

▲

THREE GENERATIONS
OF RASCHERS, 1991

home. She loved the people and the work in Sumapero. But she wasn't strong enough to live there, where they were so terribly alone. For now she would not worry about home, and that would conserve her energy.

Then came her ministry. She did not have one of those right now, either. Except to Larry. She prayed he would let go of the anguish of feeling responsible.

Shirley could feel the warmth of friends packing the chapel without looking around to meet their eyes. Larry's good friend Chuck Preston, also a south coast missionary, was reading from Psalms:

> *When my anxious thoughts multiply within me,*
> *Thy consolations delight my soul.*
>
> *Psalm 94:19, NAS*

Chip sat next to Shirley. He was thankful that school was starting and maybe life would get back to normal. In Sentani he wouldn't miss Karen and Greg so much, since they hadn't been part of his life at school. He wondered how long his parents would be so sad. He was relieved that they hadn't changed. They still seemed whole inside and they still were his mom and dad; but they were so very sad.

"Uncle" Chuck Preston continued to read from the Psalms:

> *O come, let us sing for joy to the Lord;*
> *Let us shout joyfully to the rock of our salvation.*
> *Let us come before His presence with thanksgiving;*
> *Let us shout joyfully to Him with psalms.*
> *For the Lord is a great God,*
> *And a great King above all gods,*
> *In whose hand are the depths of the earth;*
> *The peaks of the mountains are His also.*
> *The sea is His, for it was He who made it;*
> *And His hands formed the dry land.*
>
> *Psalm 95:1–5, NAS*

Larry sat on the other side of Chip. He didn't know why Karen and Greg had drowned. God made the sea, it was His, and the sea had taken them. Larry thought of verses from the 139th Psalm:

> *Thine eyes have seen my unformed substance;*
> *And in Thy book they were all written,*
> *The days that were ordained for me,*
> *When as yet there was not one of them.*
> *Psalm 139:16, NAS*

Before Greg and Karen were born, God knew how long they would live. God knew that the accident was coming, that they would go by boat, that they would go by ocean—how he wished they hadn't. But it wouldn't have mattered; it wouldn't have mattered how they went. For some reason that he might never know until heaven, the days on earth ordained for these little ones were through.

Larry knew that in the times ahead friends would try to give it meaning. Perhaps some would say, "Because of your tragedy the Lord enabled you to reach the Nafaripi"—or the Mimika, or the whomever.

He knew that the Lord would work through their circumstances for good, as He promised His people He would do. *But I will never believe for one day,* Larry whispered to God, *that you would take two of the sweetest children there ever were so that something else would happen.*

He thought of the children on their journey to Nohon in the interior just before their furlough. Karen was hardly a year old and Greg only three. Larry had been asked to preach at a tiny mission Bible school for south coast natives at Nohon. The trek took two full days by outboard, then by dugout canoe, then walking a jungle trail. The last river to cross had a single tree trunk for a bridge. The gorge was as wide as a street and plunged thirty-five feet to a foaming river. One of their native carriers walked across the fallen tree and back twice to show how well he could do it. He then put Greg on his shoulders and started across. The children trusted the natives and their parents and they made no motion or sound. The native left Greg on the far side and came back for tiny Karen. Then he crossed holding Shirley's hand, then Larry's.

It was one of so many incidents in West Irian where God had been teaching them trust, to unquestioningly trust. Somehow God would get them through this ordeal.

Larry looked down at his hands. They were strong and dexterous. He was a third generation carpenter. He loved working with tools and motors and talking with other workmen. He knew there was much work to be done for the Lord in West Irian, and that it was still his work. He longed to get back to hard work—and for his mind to quit digging a deep rut with this dark memory.

Chip watched Shirley as Bernita Preston rose to give a eulogy on the children. The thick air in the room constricted, became suffocating. What would Bernita say, all wondered. Will she be able to say it? Bernita looked at Shirley and Shirley smiled at her, melting her friend's anxieties.

The pianist began the closing hymn and all stood, united in mourning, united in perilous circumstances, united in love. They were united in commitment to a God who knew what each hurt felt like and would walk with them through each one.

And when I think that God, His Son not sparing,
Sent Him to die, I scarce can take it in;
That on the cross, my burden gladly bearing,
He bled and died to take away my sin: . . .

When Christ shall come with shout of acclamation
And take me home, what joy shall fill my heart!
Then I shall bow in humble adoration,
And there proclaim, my God, how great Thou art!

School had been in session two weeks at Faith Academy on a hilltop in Manila. It was Monday morning and all boarding as well as day students were in class, except Kathy Rascher. Since her arrival at Faith Academy Kathy had been terribly homesick for her family in West Irian. She had cried all day Sunday and now was sick in bed with a fever.

Kathy knew Faith Academy was a good school. She was an accomplished student and would do well. But she hadn't made any close friends yet except Candy Preston, who was like a big sister to her. Keith was no help because he fit in immediately.

Living together for a year on furlough had been great fun. Greg and Karen were amusing and sweet; the family had all doted on them.

Kathy sat propped up in bed in her basement dorm room, which was quiet and cool. She was working on a storybook for Greg's birthday, and the task comforted her. Just before she and Keith had left for school, their family had attended TEAM Irian's annual field conference at a mission station in the interior. Poor Greg had had the mumps. She remembered his resting what he had left of a chin on his arm, watching the other children play. He wasn't complaining. *He suffers silently like my dad does,* Kathy thought. *Sweet little Greg.*

Greg and Karen had been asleep that early morning she and Keith left for school. But the noise and commotion of the float plane at the riverbank awakened them. Shirley had grabbed them up, one in each arm, and had ran down to the riverbank so the big kids could tell them goodbye.

Many of Kathy's playmates in Kokonao and Sumapero were now marrying and carrying babies of their own. The thought made her shudder. They were bought by their husbands, their price usually about that of a pig. That thought, at least, made her glad to be where she was. She knew she would like Faith Academy once she got to know the other kids. But her dorm was a bus ride away from Keith's dorm and from the dorms of Candy and Brent Preston, their friends. The Philippines was so different from West Irian that she was acutely aware her parents were a whole country away. Kathy sat on her bed and worked on the book, lost in her memories.

As she remembered, she heard steps in the dark, quiet hallway. Mr. St. Clair, her dorm parent, appeared in the open doorway and looked at her, knocking on the door as an afterthought. He smiled at her, but seemed nervous, fidgety. "Kathy," he said. "I have to talk to you." He sat down in Kathy's desk chair and took her hand. "We've gotten news from Indonesia over the radio. Your family was in a boating accident at sea. I couldn't make out much, but I think your Mom and Dad are okay but they can't find the bodies of the baby and Keith."

Tears streamed down Kathy's face. Mr. St. Clair reached for a tissue box, close to her bed where she had used it yesterday. Her precious family. . . . "But Mr. St. Clair, Keith is here at school with me. Chip and the two babies would have been with Mom and Dad."

"Yes, I know. I didn't think that could possibly be right. Then it must be the two babies. I'm afraid I am pretty sure I heard them say two bodies. Surely we'll have more news soon, but I'm afraid that's all I know." He waited quietly, holding her hand. She had no more questions. "Keith's dorm parent will bring him over soon. We thought you'd like to spend the day together."

"Yes, thank you, Mr. St. Clair." He sat quietly until he felt his presence made no difference, then left. Kathy tried to comprehend that the dear children she had carried around as her own were gone. *At least now I'll get to see Mom and Dad,* she thought.

Keith soon met Kathy up in the rec room with a Stratego game under his arm. "Do you want to play Stra-te-go," he asked, crying. Kathy had never seen her brother cry, so her own tears came harder. "Yes," she sobbed. They sat down together in the empty room.

They each positioned their little red and blue soldiers and they played for a while in silence, each crying freely as he or she felt like it. From time to time one would think aloud. "It must have been some storm if it sank the Ebenezer."

"Poor Dad, I wonder if he feels guilty, like it was his fault."

"What will Mom do without the little kids?"

"I hope Chip is okay."

Ordinarily each would have been determined to beat the other, but in this game neither one tried to plan a strategy. It helped to be able to just go through the motions: avoiding the bombs to capture a flag.

It didn't occur to either of them that this might mean they would go back to the U.S. West Irian had been their home before Greg and Karen were born—the Lord had called them there. But they knew their family and friends in the States would worry about them.

They ate lunch at the St. Clair's, then played ping-pong on the back porch of Kathy's dorm.

In the days that followed they talked with their parents and Chip over shortwave radio, and they read together a report on the accident that Larry and Shirley put together quickly for family and fellow missionaries. Kathy was caught by the image of her parents kneeling on the beach praising God. She felt so privileged to have such a Mom and Dad. They never complained. If their food supplies were dwindling and the MAF plane was down, Mom would get sago from the natives and cook it in seventeen different ways. They'd move from one bush house to another, simply glad to be serving the Lord.

The students of Faith Academy surrounded Kathy and Keith with kindness and interest, not out of brittle duty, but genuine concern. Homesickness ceased to haunt Kathy.

Edna Rascher in St. Louis was concerned about the effect the news would have on Larry's father, Leonard, who was recovering from major surgery, and on Shirley's mother, who had had a recent heart attack. When she was convinced neither's health had been endangered by the shock, Edna set about the many tasks before her.

She managed a pyramid of details: corresponding with the family's many Stateside friends and supporting churches, collecting donations for Larry and Shirley, and purchasing and shipping replacements for items lost with the boat.

At the pinnacle was her grand idea. She would fly to Manila to make sure Kathy and Keith were okay. Leonard was doing all right and would be well taken care of by his younger son and daughter and their families, who lived nearby.

Kathy and Keith *seemed* all right to her. Both children had written their grandparents and were able to discuss in their letters what they knew of the details. "It really wasn't anybody's fault," Kathy assured them.

"We know," Edna wrote back. "The Lord led your family to West Irian and He is going to permit only what He wants to come into your lives." Edna knew that there were friends all over the world praying for them. However, she wanted to go and give Keith and Kathy some extra loving attention.

When Edna arrived she was taken to Faith Academy where Keith and Kathy were in a school assembly. One look at them and she was reassured. They were still her Kathy and Keith.

After the assembly Edna and the children went to a missionary guest house in Manila. Keith and Kathy were excited: Grandma Rascher had come just for them. They unpacked their few things and brought out Rook, which they had planned for her to play with them. After her marathon flight Edna fought to stay awake, but the cards would blur, and fall from her hands. "Don't you want to go take a nap, Grandma?" Kathy asked.

Edna wiggled a bit and repositioned her cards. "No, Honey, I want to play with you."

Edna had indeed come for the children and she spent every possible out-of-class minute with them. When Edna was moved after the weekend to another guesthouse, the school authorities suggested the kids stay in their dorms. Edna wasn't keen on the plan and had an idea. "Here I am, a former secretary, with all this time on my hands during the day. Isn't there some way I could help out in the office while the children are in school?"

Edna didn't need to offer twice. The arrangement made it practical for the children to stay in the guesthouse with her because they could all ride the bus to school together in the mornings. Public transportation was dangerous because of street riots. But Molotov cocktails in downtown Manila didn't phase Grandma Rascher—she was there for the children.

The headmaster asked Edna if she would take a group of the boarding students to the immigration office. Of course she would.

The heat was stifling, and the group arrived limp from a ride through town in the school station wagon. Edna lined up the children two by two. There was nowhere to sit and they waited and waited. Once inside the office they filled out pages of forms: Where were their parents? What were their parents doing? What would the children be doing in the Philippines and for how long?

An official offered Edna a chair in an air conditioned room down the hall. "Thank you," she said, "I'll stay with the children." In English she inquired if there was a drinking fountain in the building; no, but there was a spigot outside a half block away. But Edna couldn't lose their place in line, and she wouldn't leave any of the children. Instead, Edna and the children pooled the few coins they had between them and shared some sodas from a machine. She was impressed with the thoughtfulness of the children, no one of whom thought of trying to get bigger gulps. It seemed to her the children she knew in the States would not behave this way.

One night Edna walked with Keith and Kathy to a class party at the school gym. The gym was a couple of miles away, and Keith wanted to take a shortcut straight up the hill to it. "Grandma, could you walk up that hill?" he asked. She assured him she could. Indeed maybe she could have in Missouri, but not in the tropical heat. Soon she was falling behind.

"You kids are walking very slowly for me, but Grandma's going to have to stop and rest," she said.

"Grandma, I could carry you," Keith volunteered earnestly.

"Honey, you couldn't lift Grandma!"

"Yes I could! I could toss you over my shoulder!" Edna assured him she just needed a bit of rest. Then they went on.

Edna's mind was at rest. Keith and Kathy were

anxious about their mom and dad. They wanted to see them and talk to them, but they accepted the situation. Both had become involved in school activities. The staff and students had rallied splendidly in support of Keith and Kathy. The atmosphere of the school was warm and friendly. Edna had been made to feel welcome, and as though her presence was important. She returned to St. Louis at peace.

GRIEF DIVIDED

TEAM Irian didn't know what to do with Larry and Shirley. They knew only that they could not send the couple back to the isolation of Sumapero. The house would be full of Greg and Karen to them, and full of so very few other people.

First they were sent to spend two weeks in Manokwari. The mission field headquarters was there, as were a number of missionary families. They kept busy scrubbing and painting a Dutch barbershop which TEAM was converting to a bookstore.

If he had told the story of the accident to anyone that day, at night in Larry's dreams he was again tossing in the ocean. But in his dreams the children were not in the water. They had gone some place and would be back. Shirley dreamed she and Larry had gone somewhere and the little ones had gotten lost. She was waiting for Greg and Karen to show up again. Nights were long and hot with fitful sleep.

From Manokwari they accepted the invitation to visit south coast friends. Ruth and Cal Roesler were TEAM missionaries who had pioneered the work among Asmat tribesmen on the south coast. There was a TEAM sawmill at their station at Ayam where Larry had often prepared lumber for building projects.

Cal and Ruth were a few years older than Larry and

Shirley. Cal was a scholarly, disciplined and meticulous linguist and church planter. Ruth befriended younger missionary wives and took them under her wing.

Ruth suspected that Larry and Shirley needed to be alone to grapple with their grief. At Ayam there were the Roeslers, natives, and a dense privacy wall of jungle. Cal and Ruth moved their house helper out of his four-room house, scrubbed it down thoroughly, and prepared it for Larry and Shirley to come and stay.

Ruth had a tremendous headache the day they arrived. She confessed her anxieties to Cal. "What can we say or do to comfort them? I wish I knew what we should do."

"If you think we can do or say what they need, forget it," Cal replied. "The Lord will have to be the one to comfort them, and He will." They encouraged each other to relax and see what the Lord would do.

Larry came to Ayam with a different agenda than working hard enough to forget his troubles. He was weary of the crushing fear of being responsible. He wanted to seek the Lord and hear an answer.

Shirley fixed Larry breakfast each morning. He went to work at the sawmill, returning at noon. They ate their midday meal with Cal and Ruth. In the afternoon Larry paced the small house from wall to wall. Sometimes Ruth could hear his groans through the screens. He read—the Scriptures, a book titled *The Glory of Christ* by Wilbur M. Smith, and letters. He cried— finally. And he prayed.

Mail poured in from near and far. Shirley had little to do, and mail, especially from her children, was the high point of her days. Cal increased the frequency of his two-hour boat trips to Jawsakor to fetch it.

The letters and cards contained poems and Scripture verses and offerings of genuine love and sorrow. For Shirley it was as though the senders broke little pieces off the couple's misery and took them to themselves. In this way the size of the whole mass of their sorrow was diminished a little.

John McCain, who had built their boat the Ebenezer, ended his letter this way: "We do not know for certain whether you were in the boat which you got from us. . . . [But] if that is so my sorrow is increased for I would rather have destroyed it with my own hands than have it involved in any hurt or sorrow to you or to your family."

One particular letter Larry and Shirley read aloud together over and over because of the encouragement and hope they drew from it. It was from D.J. DePree:

"Dear Larry and Shirley:

". . . These communications from you indicate how marvelously the grace of God and the comfort of God has been given to you. It reminds us of Genesis 23 in which we read about Abraham at Sarah's death 'getting up from before his dead' and going on with the responsibilities of life.

"The world says 'time heals all things' but actually it does not. The triumph of Christ over death is our triumph.

". . . I feel led to give you my experience with one verse of scripture. It is Luke 24:30. [*And it came about that when He had reclined at table with them, He took the bread and blessed it, and breaking it, He began giving it to them. (NAS)*]

"In December, 1952, our [daughter] Barbara and Audrey De Jonge . . . were asphyxiated in a motel in Daytona Beach. It happened on the night of Barbara's 21st birthday.

"Soon after that I had to be in London to help the British Gideons 'bible' the hotels in London in preparation for the coronation of Queen Elizabeth. While there in March of 1953, at a lunch table on Monday noon, there was inquiry about this from the four men who were taking me to lunch. Three of them were older men. One was a younger man. After reciting what led to the sudden death of these two girls, the older men were speechless but the younger man, William Thompson, told us of a message that he had heard the evening before by a layman in a Hall in London. It was on the picture in Luke 24:30. This greatly comforted me and stimulated private study.

"Nine times, I discovered, we see this same picture in the Scriptures. . . . In each of them we see with our mind's eye our Lord taking bread; blessing it; breaking it; giving it.

"First of all it's a picture of Himself. He took a body. I Timothy 3:16. He blessed this body. It was the most blessed body that ever walked the earth. On the cross that body was broken. Galatians 2:20 and John 10:11. Then He gave. Because of His resurrection, eternal life became distributable to all who would receive it. II Peter 1:4 and John 10:28.

"The second picture we see is what He did for you and me:

"#1 - He took us out of Adam, out of darkness, out of condemnation, out of the realm of death, out of the way of perishing.

"#2 - He blesses us as we never could have been blessed in any other way. He blesses our families. He blesses our activities. He blesses our total life.

"#3 - He breaks us. He breaks our wills. He breaks our plans, our tempers, our habits, our appetites, our bodies, our pocketbooks, our families. He has the right to do it.

"#4 - He gives us to others in a needy world.

"When He took us it was Ownership. When He blesses us it is Sponsorship. When He breaks us it's Lordship. When He gives us, it's Partnership.

"Many times in Gideon meetings around the

country, in the devotional periods, this truth was brought out with blessings . . . "

Many other friends shared with them the depths and the blessings of their own remembered sorrows.

Ruth made the meals they shared as special as she could. One afternoon she baked a cake, expecting Larry and Shirley that evening for supper. Shirley came into the kitchen to help Ruth. Shirley had on a flowered cotton shirtwaist dress and new sandals. Larry wore a freshly ironed short-sleeved shirt and slacks. Their outfit had not yet arrived from Michigan, but their sizes had been broadcast over the radio to other missionaries. Clothing had been filtering in to them from The Missionary Fellowship all over West Irian. They were still waiting for new glasses from the U.S. Their bruises had healed and both looked more rested.

Shirley stood looking at the cake. Tears welled in her eyes. Ruth put her arm around her friend and waited for her to talk. "Today is Gregory's birthday," she said quietly, trying to smile at Ruth. "He would be four today."

As the darkness closed in the two couples talked at the table by candlelight. The cake was eaten. They talked about little Gregory and how he had been "pure Rascher." At the annual conference, before Greg came down with mumps, each morning he visited the man in charge of serving Coca-Colas. "Could I please just have a sip?" he would ask, dimples showing on his chubby face. Larry and Shirley shared many of their wonderful memories.

Over the course of a month at Ayam, Larry received the relief he had been seeking.

"The glory of God is best seen as Christ is dying on the cross," Larry told Cal Roesler about his study in *The Glory of Christ.* "Every truth of life is best seen and understood as we look at the cross. If you want to understand surrender, look at Christ on the cross. If you want to know commitment, look at Christ as He died. And if you want to know what it is to trust God when you don't understand, Jesus shows that at the cross.

"Jesus died by faith. It was as if Jesus said to His Father, 'This is new to Me. In My eternal existence I have never been separated from You. I don't understand it. But You don't ever make a mistake, and into Your hands I commend My spirit.'

"From a human perspective, Christ yielded not only to the will of the Father, but to the wisdom of the Father. Even in something Jesus couldn't explain, He could trust His Father.

"I don't know why Karen and Greg went with us," said Larry, his voice rising. "I don't know why we couldn't fly, or why the boat broke up. I don't know why the waves were so high.

"But if Jesus could trust His unknown into the Father's hands, so can I. Someday, when we're with Jesus too, then we'll understand."

The two men bowed their heads and prayed together, Cal taller and more slender and dark-haired, distinguished looking; Larry with his shoulders visibly relaxing. Larry sighed as he began to pray. They were two friends who talked to God as regularly and as easily as to other people.

"I'm going to quit climbing this wall, Lord," Larry prayed, "as to why we went out there and why this happened. We all have some things in our lives that we don't understand—and that we don't need to know. You are my Father, and you never make a mistake. I'm going to know all about it someday. It's going to be just as clear as anything we've ever understood.

"Father, we thank you for every minute of every day you gave us to serve you in West Irian, including July 24, 1971."

The pain continued to haunt Larry, but not the awful burden of feeling responsible. He was ready to get back to work.

There was drought on the south coast that fall. Thick, acrid smoke from smoldering forest fires kept the MAF planes grounded. Pilot Herb Morgan tended to other projects, like helping Larry revamp and install an inboard/outboard motor in the boat given by Mr. DePree. The motor had been given to Larry by Costas Macris, an Irian missionary with Regions Beyond Missionary Union. Larry had no idea at the time just how much active service this boat would receive in the Rascher household.

Herb and his wife Eloise invited Larry and Shirley to visit them at Jawsakor, where the MAF Cessnas were fitted with floats for service in the swamps.

Eloise was a young mother with an open home and a big heart. She hoped that they could minister to these friends by letting them talk. And talk they did. The two couples shared some good jokes together, as they had in the past. Now it seemed that one meal together they laughed and the next they cried.

It didn't take Eloise long to pick up on two things which Shirley very much needed to do. Eloise was cooking one morning as Shirley helped in the kitchen. Timmy Frazier, the son of missionary neighbors, came in. As was obviously his custom, he pulled a kitchen chair up to the stove and began "helping" Eloise.

The similarities between Timmy and Greg, who loved to cook, were more than Shirley could handle. She left the room quickly and Eloise followed her.

"Shirley, you go back by the generator and you have a good, long cry. No one will hear you or bother you. I've done it myself a time or two." Eloise went back into the house. She didn't see Shirley again until evening. With need number one taken care of, Eloise dealt with need number two.

"You need to take Chipper and go see Keith and Kathy in Manila for Thanksgiving," Eloise said over supper.

For a few moments there were only fork and spoon scratchings. Larry looked at Shirley with an expression that had become common to him. He searched her face to see if the comment opened a wound.

"There's no way we could afford it," Shirley began. "We just flew back from furlough; we just bought our outfit. Wouldn't it be selfish to ask for money we don't have to use when they'll be coming home for Christmas?"

"Of course not! You need to be together as a family. Kathy and Keith need you. I believe the Lord wants to bring you together for healing. Get in touch with TEAM in the States. Maybe there's a way."

Shirley sighed, and Eloise sensed that her friend had been awaiting permission to try to go. Larry agreed to try, but he hoped Shirley would not be disappointed.

TEAM responded by depositing a grant of $2000 to their account—the money needed for the trip. And as the years passed, repayment was never requested, even when they asked about it.

A letter from Faith Academy was further confirmation they should make the trip. It was from Kathy and Keith's teachers. "They're doing okay," it read, "but it would be good if you could come."

Meanwhile, with Herb Morgan, Larry caught the vision for a new work. It was not like Sumapero. They would not be pouring out their lives to an unreached tribe. But it involved lots of building. And it was on the south coast, at Senggo. From there they could make frequent visits to the Nafaripi.

At Senggo TEAM Irian wanted to build a large mission station. There they would relocate Dr. Dresser and the TEAM hospital, which had been washed out by the ocean at Pirimapun. They would hack an airstrip out of the jungle so that Herb and other MAF pilots could service the station. Herb helped Larry tramp through the marshy ground and select the best site. A hospital, the doctor's home, a guesthouse, and homes for other TEAM missionaries would be built.

At TEAM Irian's quarterly field council meeting that fall, Larry and Shirley were reassigned to the building work at Senggo.

❧

At the airport in Manila, Larry, Shirley and Chip didn't have to search long for Kathy and Keith. As they walked from the plane to the terminal they spotted them immediately on a second story balcony overlooking the landing area. "Mom! Dad! Chip!" They waved and yelled, oblivious to the amused Filipinos around them. Shirley cried as they hurried into the terminal: with relief, with joy, and with the shedding of an undefinable weight.

They met in a hallway and hugged each other; quickly the tears were gone and they were just themselves, together again. Only now the family all seemed a little more grown up. They no longer had little children with them—and their loss had aged them all.

All details had been carefully planned by the staff at Faith Academy: the children's transportion to the airport, transportation from the airport, accommodations in missionary housing, a meal that evening. It came together so smoothly that they were riding a magic carpet. They concentrated on enjoying the presence of one another and on catching up.

They were all exiting a long, dark tunnel. They ate together and played together. Keith had taken up running, so Chip ran with him each day after school. They attended all school functions together. Larry preached in Manila. Friends took them to Subic Bay to see where the U.S. Navy was refitting boats for service in Vietnam.

They shopped together in the two- and three-story buildings of cubicle-sized shops downtown. In one shop Larry had a mother's ring custom-made for Shirley. Five gemstones were set in a silver band, birthstones of the children. Opals of different hues for Kathy and Keith were on the outside. Then came Karen's aquamarine, Chip's red garnet, and Greg's olive green peridot. The merchant had never heard of a mother's ring. At first he set the stones up on top of the band. "No," said Shirley. "It's too flashy and I'll lose one." By the time they left Manila the ring had been reset with the stones in the band. It was just right, and it was beautiful.

Larry and Shirley had established a rule for themselves soon after the accident: they would not talk about the accident unless someone asked them. They did not like to feel they were dramatizing the tragedy of their children's death. And they did not want to play upon the sympathies of others. They would certainly talk about it, but only if asked.

Kathy and Keith didn't ask. Or at least they didn't ask for details when Larry stumbled through pieces of the accident with them, weeping. Kathy was stunned, not so much by the story as by the fact that Larry was crying. Her daddy didn't cry. *He must have loved Greg and Karen very much,* she thought, *and he must also love the rest of us deeply.*

For their part, Larry and Shirley could not have gotten through the whole story even if the children had asked them. Keith and Kathy had read the written account that Larry and Shirley sent to family and friends soon after the accident. That would have to suffice for now.

They did talk freely together about memories of Karen and Greg and all the cute and sweet things they said and did.

Chip talked to Kathy about the accident only once.

They were in Sumapero for Christmas a month after the Manila visit. It was a good family Christmas, but a hard time of finally saying goodbye to life with the Nafaripi. "All of our women have lost children, *Tuan*. Why do you have to go?" Chief Esapa and others pleaded with them. They grieved with them, but didn't understand why this should take them away.

"No, we can't stay here yet," Larry replied, wincing at the gaze of his tall friend Esapa, for whom Larry had great respect. The loss of this vision, this work, was crushing atop the loss of the children. "But we'll keep things in our home here because we'll come back and visit often."

They found that in their absence from Sumapero some of the Nafaripi had become discouraged and had fallen away from their faith. Larry taught the men and Shirley met separately with the women, who tended to be timid and withdrawn.

Jonas and Nimrod had faithfully continued teaching school in Sumapero. Jonas had grown to love the Nafaripi now that he was responsible over them, and he was committed to staying. He had taken a Biaker wife, too, which helped to settle him there. Jonas and Nimrod worked well together.

An airstrip was being built at Sumapero, to link it more securely to other stations. Larry helped work on it at Christmas. Herb Morgan assured Larry he'd fly in to check on the people of Sumapero as often as he could.

Chip and Kathy stood along the banks of the Cemara River at Sumapero one evening that Christmas. They were having one of their good talks like old times in Kokonao. Chip always looked to Kathy for spiritual guidance and good advice.

They stood quietly for a while. Chip stared into a current in the otherwise sluggish brown water. "Kathy, you should have seen the boat!" Chip said softly, almost as if to himself. "The waves were so high it was standing on end and then it came slapping down." Chip showed Kathy with his hands. He glanced at her for a moment, as if looking for an answer. That was all he said.

SENGGO

A native house had been built for Larry and Shirley in Senggo. It had five large rooms, *atap* walls and roof, and a short life expectancy. Larry would build Shirley a proper house when work slowed down. But they felt at home and expectant for the first time in many months.

"Isn't this wonderful!" Shirley said as they lay talking in the dark one night. Bulky shadows surrounded the bed, but they weren't monsters. They were piles of "Rascher stuff" at last.

Their outfit had arrived from the States, and Larry had made several trips to Jawsakor in the Moppi boat to get it. By this their third outfit, they knew what they needed to live comfortably and work effectively on the south coast. New electric tools, purchased in Michigan, were piled in the living room behind two new Herman Miller chairs. In back of the house a large generator kept company with the new Maytag washer. They now had a comfortable rocking chair, although it stood empty more than they'd planned. A beautiful large desk, a gift from D.J. DePree, doubled as a dining table since Larry had no separate study. Pictures hung on the walls.

Out in the *gudang*, Justinus, a young Nafaripi man they had brought from Sumapero to be their house

151

helper, sat roasting sago over his small fire. He had helped the *tuan* unload many foreign western things today. He was weary and was missing his own people in Sumapero. He was also missing growing to manhood in his own village, where he was somebody important.

The Raschers had American next-door neighbors. Pat Moore, a lab technician, and Helen Edds, a nurse, were TEAM missionaries who would also take part in founding the large mission station at Senggo. They, too, were temporarily living in a bush house. The Dresser's house was a distance off through jungle, near the site of the new airstrip.

Senggo felt just civilized enough. In the jungle beyond Senggo lay the villages of the Citak tribe, unacquainted with the outside world or the gospel. The highlands to the north of Senggo, where the rivers of its swamplands were formed, had yet to be surveyed. Senggo was a good mix of camaraderie, challenge, and hard work.

The only problem Shirley could see was that the ground at Senggo was a huge brown sponge. Never in her years on the south coast had mud been quite so inescapable.

"I'm not coming out of here for a long time," Shirley thought aloud to Larry. "Not after what we had to walk through to get here. Lawrence, do you realize how many different beds we've slept in since July?" Larry laughed. He was quiet, but Shirley could tell he was listening.

"I told Eloise about the mud and that I wasn't coming out. She said the Lord must have something very special for me here."

They both laughed, but Larry hoped that Eloise was right.

乚

Sunday night
February 13, 1972

Dear Friends,

Today began as a fairly normal Sunday. Pat and I had breakfast, washed the dishes, and left for church with the Raschers about 8:00 a.m. The Raschers moved into the house next door to us a week ago yesterday, on February 5. Larry has been a big help with supervising the clearing and construction around us. He gets right in and works along with the rest of the men, and both he and Shirley have been a real blessing to us.

After the service in Indonesian in the village, we all went over to the Dressers' house for a service in English (just the missionaries, nobody else around here speaks English). We sang, prayed, and listened to a taped message from a church in California. Around noon we left the Dressers' house and started home. Our houses are about 15 to 30 minutes through the jungle from the Dressers' house, depending on who is doing the walking! Ken and Larry can probably do it in 15 minutes, but for the rest of us it is closer to half an hour. We had scarcely left the Dressers' house when we heard something that sounded like a gun being fired off in the distance and wondered what in the world it was! The local people don't have guns; they do their hunting with bows and arrows and/or spears. I thought that perhaps it was a crocodile hunter (usually Indonesian or Chinese).

As we walked toward home, Shirley commented that she was too tired to cook lunch and decided they would just have sandwiches for lunch, and after they rested a bit she would cook a meal for supper. Pat and I were both feeling pretty tired too, and so decided that might be a good idea for us as well. We were planning to have another Indonesian service at 4:00 p.m. and could eat after that. As we got closer to the clearing in the jungle where we live we heard an unusual amount of squealing and yelling and wondered again just what was taking place. Could it be a big fight or tribal warfare in the jungle near us? Before we had time to think or discuss it much further, an Irianese man appeared and shouted, *"Rumah terbakar!"* House is on fire! We didn't know whose house it was or how bad it might be.

Larry broke into a run and I took out behind him. We had been walking carefully, avoiding mud as much as we could; but now we ran not heeding the mud and a time or two I sank almost up to my knees. Larry was a fair distance ahead of me, and I was about halfway between him and the other two ladies. At that point we didn't know whether it was our house or theirs, or both, or how bad it might be. Soon I was within sight of flames and smoke. I didn't get too good of a look, but its appeared to be the Raschers' house, which was right next to ours. I couldn't see for sure whether it was both houses or not. Larry turned around and saw me and shouted, "Stay with Shirley," and so I knew it must be pretty bad. I turned around and retraced my steps to where Pat and Shirley were coming up behind me and said to Shirley, "I think it's your house." The first thing she said was, "Oh, my precious babies' pictures!" Their only pictures of their two children who went to be with the Lord last July were in that house (the others were lost in her purse in the boat accident). My heart ached for her and for Larry. I put my arms around her and the three of us stood there and wept for a few minutes. Larry came up and said as gently as he could, "It's our house, Honey."

We walked on through the jungle then, until we were all in sight of the flaming house, which by then was a total loss—burned to the ground, not a wall or a floor left, just the *tiangs*, foundation poles on which the house had stood, were still erect in the midst of ashes. I saw the refrigerator fall through the floor before that section completely burned away. They had brought quite a few of their things here as they expected to be here for a long time in their work with building the new hospital complex, and all the new buildings here, and the airstrip, etc. Their lovely new Philips stove, a brand-new record player, tape recorder, records, and music tapes were all lost, as well as things like their passports, clothing, linens, pots and pans, and all things one uses in day-to-day living. The new Maytag washer had melted. Larry had a new Bible in the house, too. All they had left was what they were wearing. The noise we had heard, by the way, had been things exploding in the fire.

If it had been any other day of the week, some-one would almost definitely have been around and perhaps something could have been salvaged, but with all of us and all the Irianese workers away, it was too far gone to rescue anything by the time anyone got there. One of the men was running around with a wash basin he had found on my back porch, but of course, there was nothing any-body could do. When it stopped, there were only ashes left.

We all came on over to our house (Pat's and mine) and sent a message to Ken Dresser to let him know what had happened. At that point we couldn't stop to think about being tired and decided we'd better have a proper meal after all. So we cooked and ate lunch. Both Larry and Shirley took it well. After the first tears were past they were even able to laugh. As we prayed at the dinner table, Larry thanked God for His love and His sovereignty.

They decided it would probably be best for them to go to Jawsakor today if possible, as they had a few clothes there, and also since they could stay in the Fraziers' house temporarily (Fraziers are on vacation in the mountains). This would be easier on them than crowding in with the Dressers or with us, and especially so since they had some of their own clothing there. Ken called MAF and made arrangements for the float plane pilot Herb to come and get them around 3:30 p.m.

It's about an hour's walk to the river to get on the plane, and so we got up from the dinner table and set out immediately for the river, as it was about 2:15 then. I went along to keep Shirley company, while Larry went back to Dressers' house before starting for the river. They had a boy from Sumapero (their usual station) with them, living in the back of their house. He, too, had lost everything and so Larry wanted to make arrangements for him with Ken before leaving. As we started out through the jungle once again, the sky was dark and threatening, and we had to watch for possible falling trees as we made our way over the narrow trail. Trees frequently fall during storms, as their roots aren't very deep around here.

And so tonight it seems strangely silent as I sit by my kerosene lamp writing this letter. Although they have only lived next to us for a week, we had gotten used to having someone around besides ourselves, to seeing lights next door at night, and to hearing music floating from their windows. Next to the pictures, I think Larry will miss his music the most. Do pray especially for them as they emerge from this new trial, while still feeling very realistically the loss of their little ones. Pray for the children, too, as they learn of this new loss. Kathy and Keith are in Faith Academy in the Philippines, and Chipper is in M.K. school in Sentani. . . .

Sincerely in Christ,

Helen Edds

ॐ

Eloise Morgan and their two little daughters were resting when the call came over the radio from Ken Dresser. Eloise overheard the conversation in the kitchen and got up from bed so quickly she was dizzy for a moment. She stood in back of Herb's chair with her hands on his shoulders, and listened.

"Herb, I can't believe it. All their things they had just unpacked. Poor Shirley. What in the world will they do?"

Herb and Eloise prayed for their friends. When Herb left to ready the plane, Eloise picked up the girls' toys from the living room. She walked the elevated board-walk between their houses to open the Frazier house and see that it was ready. She sent her house girl to the village to ask the Frazier's house girl to come help Shirley as long as they stayed. She then asked a young native man to bring the Raschers' only remaining drum from the MAF storehouse to the Frazier house.

Eloise had koladi chips and lemonade ready when they arrived. There was no unpacking or settling in to do. They sat in the Morgan's living room and talked. Eloise thought they looked tired, but otherwise Larry and Shirley seemed fine.

"How did it happen?" Herb asked.

"I don't know, Herb," said Larry. You know those *atap* houses are tinder boxes. It could be that the wick from either the kerosene stove or refrigerator was too close to the wall. We're burning brush on the airstrip now and I guess it could have been sparks blown over from there, but that's hard to imagine.

"Or it could have been Justinus. He's staying in the *gudang* and I've told him over and over he shouldn't go to sleep with his fire burning, even though I gave him a fifty-five-gallon drum lid to lay it on. He denies that he did, but he may just be frightened. He's really having a hard time. Maybe we shouldn't have brought him with us. I asked Ken to arrange to get him back to Sumapero."

"I don't think we'll ever know how it started," said Shirley. "But belongings are really the least of our worries. I'm just glad no one was hurt."

Eloise glanced at Shirley's hands and noticed with relief that she was wearing the mother's ring Larry had bought for her in Manila. The five oval stones were simple yet striking. Shirley noticed Eloise looking at her ring. "Do you know this is the only day I put this on first thing in the morning?" said Shirley, sliding the ring from side to side on her finger.

"The worst of it is losing our photos of Greg and Karen and our snapshots from furlough."

"Does anyone in the States have negatives?" Eloise asked.

"Yes, I think so, somewhere. Edna can find them if anyone can. Poor Edna. We sure keep her busy. Both of us are missing our glasses again. And the new Bible they just sent Lawrence. And our address list and passports and birth certificates and marriage license. Hey Lawrence, do you suppose anyone will believe we really are who we say we are?"

A supporting church in Canada sent the Morgans tapes of its Sunday morning services. The Morgans listened to one each Sunday night. It didn't matter that the July series of sermons might get to them in November.

Eloise lit a kerosene lamp on the living-room table and Herb put in the Sunday tape. First the choir sang.

They all knew the hymn and sang too: *God Leads Us Along.* Larry sang by far the loudest, and well, so it didn't really matter what the others sounded like.

> *In shady green pastures,*
> *So rich and so sweet,*
> *God leads His dear children along;*
> *Where the water's cool flow*
> *Bathes the weary one's feet,*
> *God leads His dear children along.*
>
> *Some through the water,*
> *Some through the flood,*
> *Some through the fire,*
> *But all through the blood.*
>
> *Some through great sorrow,*
> *But God gives a song,*
> *In the night seasons*
> *And all the day long.*

The couples couldn't finish the song for laughing. They laughed and laughed. They laughed away anxiety about tomorrow and next week. They laughed at the tragic irony of their situation. They laughed and laughed because life goes on. Larry and Shirley had learned that well. Life goes on. They had been through the worst—this fire was not nearly the worst—and life would go on.

"Rascher," said Herb, "you're the only guy I know who's been through all of them." They laughed some more. They listened to the sermon, but broke into it to talk whenever they felt like it. Then the couples parted for bed.

PART TWO

THE NORTH COAST

A TIME TO REAP

TEAM Irian had decided what to do with Larry and Shirley, at least for a year. After the fire at Senggo, the TEAM Irian field council in Irian Jaya (the name the Indonesian government settled upon for West Irian) reassigned them to Manokwari on the north coast. The Ron Hill family was leaving on a year's furlough, and the Raschers could stay in their home. Larry would assume Ron's duties in TEAM Irian's field office in Manokwari. He would purchase supplies for missionaries in the Bird's Head, hire teachers for TEAM schools, represent TEAM Irian in government matters, and work with the mission's two Manokwari churches. Shirley would do the clerical work and operate TEAM's bookstore. Helen Edds, from Senggo, would serve as bookkeeper. "We've got to get you out of dangerous places," the council said.

The fire closed the chapter of their lives on the south coast of Irian Jaya. It took a specific outfit to be able to live and work effectively with primitive people in the middle of a swamp. The Raschers no longer had these items, and it would have taken a lot of time and money to re-assemble them. On the north coast they could use the Hills' equipment and household items while they slowly assembled their own belongings, from the generosity of fellow missionaries and from family and supporters in the States. They hurt for the Nafaripi at Sumapero who were without a resident missionary, with the work there young but well begun.

Manokwari was the fourth largest city in Irian Jaya, with 15,000 coastal natives, Chinese and Indonesians. Larry and Shirley felt inadequate for the new job. Larry was comfortable in the swamps living with native people and loving them and teaching them, moving here and there on building projects as a jack-of-all-trades. He loved the freedom, the people, the country, and Shirley loved their life there as well. Larry wasn't sure of his skills at office work and church planting. *His strength is made perfect in our weakness.* They were depending upon this.

The move represented major changes: From swamps to white sand beaches. From primitive tribesmen to civilized nationals. From tribal evangelism to city church planting. From shopping trips via boat or float plane to browsing in neighborhood bakeries and *tokos*. The move meant a much easier way of life. They could even buy Dad's Root Beer™.

Larry and Shirley and the three children spent two golden months in a missionary house near the Bible school at Saowi before the Hills left and their house and outfit became available. For that summer, TEAM Irian kept Larry's responsibilities at a minimum. When he did have a building project, Keith and Chip went along.

The family picnicked on the beaches. Kathy and Shirley played checkers with giant plastic checkers and a square beach towel which had a checker board printed on one side. Larry and the boys dove and spearfished along the coral reefs. Keith and Chip rode the waves in outrigger canoes. They paddled out past the breakers and rode in on the swells. They all stuck closer together than in past school vacations. They grew accustomed to their new family size and shape: the folks and three big kids. They were close friends.

Larry bought a car, an old creamed-colored Volkswagen bug that they had to push to start, and they went on drives to villages along the dirt roads. Larry was the first missionary in Manokwari to own his own car. He took some ribbing, but others soon followed suit. Whenever Larry passed nationals he knew walking along the road, he gave them a ride.

The family played volleyball and soccer with Bible school students at Saowi, and many nights the family lingered around the dinner table after dark. They learned that the accident cast a shadow none of them could ever elude. The shadow would loom large and dark at times, and at other times be like an imperceptibly thin film. They would always be the Raschers who had lost their children, their siblings.

Almost immediately Larry and Shirley were called upon to help comfort people in tragedy. A Christian national came running to their house one night. He took Larry and Shirley to his home-on-stilts over the ocean. Inside, his wife held their little son who had fallen through the board walkway and had drowned. The child's body was deteriorating rapidly, but the mother moaned and rocked it as a casket was being prepared for burial. Shirley saw again, with aching heart, the little corpse they had seen at intervals on the crest of waves. She wept with the mother and comforted her.

By the time the kids went back to school, Larry and Shirley were feeling more whole, refreshed and ready for the whirl of events to follow.

Larry took charge of plans Ron Hill had made for the largest evangelistic meetings ever held in Manokwari. The necessary signatures of government and church officials had been procured on the permission forms.

An evangelistic team was coming from Jakarta to lead the meetings: Petrus Anthony, an evangelist; Eddy Karamoy, a guitarist famous throughout Indonesia;

song leader Martinus Noya; and two young women, Atje (Ace) and Paula, who sang duets. This was the most auspicious group ever assembled on a covered platform at the ball field in the center of Manokwari. Enthusiastic members of TEAM's two Manokwari churches, Wosi and Fanindi, prayed for the meetings and served as the choir, the ushers, the custodians and the counselors.

The men of the evangelistic team stayed with the Raschers and the two women stayed with Helen Edds. They all ate together at the Raschers'. The house was filled with talk and laughter and music and delicious food.

With a lively speaker and pleasant music, and no competing activities, crowds came: 3,000 the first and last days, and 500 to 1000 the middle three days, when they had to stand or squat on the muddy ballfield in pouring rain. Many listened from their homes. The women's duets were such a hit that in Manokwari scores of newborn girl babies were named Atje or Paula. During those days many people heard for the first time who Jesus Christ was, what He had done for them, and how they could know Him.

These were amazing times to be a missionary in Irian Jaya. For a couple of dark years, local missionaries had said it was as if Satan had had a temper tantrum. Now great strongholds of evil, particularly in the highlands, had broken open. Whole tribes in the mountains were burning their fetishes and asking to be taught about the living God. The meetings in Manokwari also gave coastal tribes the opportunity to hear about Christ.

As the meetings commenced a delegation of disgruntled coastal mountain natives walked the many miles to Manokwari to see *Bapak* Rascher and the evangelistic team. Why were these wonderful meetings all to be conducted in Indonesian? Could they not have meetings given in their languages as well?

Larry promised them that the meetings on Saturday, the final day, would be held especially for them, with interpreters for the Hattam, Minikion and Meyak languages. He made the necessary arrangements.

On Friday nearly 3,000 nationals streamed down the mountainside, along the coast, and into the town of Manokwari. They choked the roads and struck fear into local merchants, who had never seen mountain people in these numbers. With them the mountain people had brought relatives so that their kinsmen could hear the gospel. They built small cooking fires and slept in huddles in and around Manokwari, quietly awaiting their special meetings on Saturday. They were proud of the great host of believers their numbers displayed. But they were fearful as well.

They had come down out of the mountains, they told *Bapak* Rascher, and along the coast toward Manokwari through the village of Maruni. There were three Christian families in Maruni. They had been harassed by the other villagers and forced to move across the river.

The people of Maruni were annoyed with the procession of mountain Christians along their quiet path. They had put *obatan*, evil medicine, on the path as the mountain Christians came through. "Please pray for our people at these meetings, *Bapak* Rascher, so that they won't get sick or die." They had seen the evil powers of this magic. Even though they were now Christians, these natives were afraid.

In Tanahmerah, another coastal village, the villagers had laughed at them as the mountain people passed. "If we see the blind and deaf healed, then we'll believe," they said.

There was no storm Friday night, although it had rained much of the week; but a single bolt of lightning pierced the tropical night, followed by a deep roar and rumbling—longer than thunder, longer than an earthquake. The thousands gathered in Manokwari had been through earthquakes, but nothing like this. Few slept in trembling Manokwari.

The Hill house where the Raschers stayed was built of cement blocks on a hill overlooking Manokwari Bay. Larry and Shirley stood at their front window the next morning, discussing the amazing sight before them across the bay. The side of a mountain lake had given way, releasing a massive torrent of jungle growth and water and mud to the ocean below. At the shore the mud flow was at least four miles wide. Below this mud, the village of Maruni and its inhabitants were now buried completely, except that on the other side of the river the deluge did not begin until just below the homes of the Christians.

Saturday was a day of jubilee. Seventy-five coastal mountain natives, brought by believing relatives, accepted Jesus Christ as Savior, whose medicine was stronger than *obatan*. After the meetings in their languages, the mountain natives sang and clapped their way back through the city streets and toward the mountains, a Volkswagen in the throng. The scar on the mountain across Manokwari Bay would serve as a reminder for generations of the folly of Maruni and the blessing of God. And from that day the people of the village of Tanahmerah believed in Jesus Christ.

The months after the evangelistic meetings in Manokwari demanded every bit of energy and wisdom, patience and love that Larry and Shirley had to give. But it was the work a missionary longs for, and it left little room for loneliness or indulged sorrow.

The two TEAM churches in Manokwari held classes for new believers and assimilated many of them into their congregations. The Wosi and Fanindi churches doubled in size. Two new churches sprang up in Manokwari, others in villages outside of town. Tribal groups formed their own churches and worshipped together, whether in the city of Manokwari or outside it. During the meetings, 167 people from the Manokwari area had professed new faith in Jesus Christ. The numbers grew as these new believers shared what they'd learned with their family members. Never had Larry and Shirley enjoyed the work more than they did teaching and getting to know these new believers.

There were weekly men's meetings and women's classes and baptismal classes, many led by Bob or Shirley Lenz, missionaries at the Bible school at Saowi, or by Larry or Shirley. The people were hungry to learn more. Men came to the women's classes and women came to the men's, and people attended the baptismal classes who had long since been baptised. Larry and Shirley were exhausted, but exuberant. The aching spots in their hearts throbbed less insistently, at fewer and more private times.

The movement toward Christ met with persecution— just enough to fan the flames. The Dutch Reformed Church had extensively evangelized the north coast of Irian Jaya. But the churches had settled into a dead orthodoxy, with no emphasis on personal faith in Jesus Christ. Animistic practices had been woven back into the rituals. However, though dead to the faith, these churches did not give up members easily.

One day Larry went to preach at the nearby village of a friend, Inawasep, a carpenter. Inawasep came to Larry's house early that day. "*Tuan*, you had better not come. The village is angry that you are coming."

Drawn to the challenge, Larry did go and preached to forty villagers in Inawasep's *gaba gaba* home. Three times as many people surrounded the house and taunted them. They ranted and rattled sticks along the palm-stalk walls to create a racket. They threw rocks on the corrugated aluminum roof.

It was quite a show, but the house held up and none of the believers were hurt. Eventually many more villagers were won to belief in Christ. The attitude was "If these were won to belief in Christ. The attitude was "If these guys are willing to stand up under this, there must be something to it."

Cargo cults presented a further challenge to the new churches. Cargo cults are present on many Pacific islands, and are strong on islands off the north coast of Irian Jaya near Manokwari. They are materialistic cults spawned by the advent of trade ships from the West carrying riches and undreamed-of inventions and technologies.

Each island tribe believes they live in the center of where the world began. They must then rationalize in some way how Western nations, rather than they themselves, acquired the secrets to such wealth. Dreams and visions pervade the cults: dreams of how they, too, will inherit goods; visions concerning practices they must follow to be sure the dreams come true. Cultists often embrace Christianity as a confirmation of their cultic beliefs. The cult thereby infiltrates the Christian churches on the islands.

One version of the cargo cult from the natives of Biak, an island 125 miles east of Manokwari, goes like this: A Biaker noticed that food kept disappearing from his garden. One night he slept in his garden, and awoke to find a pig eating his vegetables. He followed the pig to a cave. In the cave the pig began talking to the Biaker, and told him he had the power of eternal life. He shared the secret of this power with the Biaker.

The Biaker immediately became afflicted with a skin disease and was thrown out of his village. *His own people rejected him.*

He wandered to another village. There he found the chief's lovely virgin daughter walking alone on the beach. He threw a papaya at her. It hit her on the breast and she became pregnant. *A virgin shall be with child.*

The chief was furious. He lined up all the men of the village to determine who was guilty. The Biaker with daughter fled with the villagers in pursuit.

The Biaker drew a canoe in the sand on the beach and it became real. As the villagers drew back in amazement, the Biaker said they were going away to the West but would return to bring them happiness and wealth and eternal life if they would follow certain rules. *I go to prepare a place for you.* They were not to eat pork or sweet potatoes. And he said that when he returned he would have white skin.

For a hundred years many Biakers have believed in this vision. There is a particular island close to Biak where he is to return. The island is now frequented by tourist ships. The Biakers take the Westerners' interest in this island as a further confirmation.

Many new Christian believers around Manokwari brought into the churches invisible baggage from the cargo cults. But it wasn't until later that Larry and Shirley became aware of it.

Shirley had a dilemma. She now managed a little Dutch barbershop-turned-bookstore in the heart of Manokwari. But she knew nothing about ordering or selling books—until one midnight. The Lord brought to her door an "angel", a messenger, in the slight, aged figure of Ibu Chang.*

Ibu Chang had been an independent American missionary to China as a young woman in 1919. She had married a Chinese man who died soon after their wedding. She kept his name. When Christian missionaries were expelled from China she came to Indonesia and eventually to Jayapura, capital city of Irian Jaya, where she sold books each day from a stall in the marketplace. She lived to get books—especially books

* For the full story of Ibu [Grace] Chang read *Called to the Hard Places*, published by Christian Literature Crusade.

on Christian themes and Bibles—into the hands of the Irianese.

Larry and Shirley had met Ibu Chang while they were shopping in Jayapura. Ibu Chang heard about Shirley's new bookstore. She had been on a boat which docked at Manokwari in the middle of the night. Through inquiring of natives who sat talking in clusters on the road, she found her way to the Raschers' home.

They talked until the wee hours of the morning, exhausting both Shirley's questions and the elderly lady, who stayed as their guest. Shirley took this encouragement as directly from the Lord. He had restored her husband and He had given Shirley a home—and a ministry.

She began her business slowly but enthusiastically. She found that there was a brisk market for school textbooks, which students had to buy. Besides textbooks, she stocked Indonesian titles recommended by Ibu Chang. She offered *Light of Life* Bible correspondence courses, which had been developed in India, and Billy Graham books for the few customers who wanted books in English. Eventually she branched out to cassettes of Indonesian hymns, calendars, and comics of Old Testament stories.

She employed Bible school students and a Wosi church leader as helpers. But whenever possible Shirley worked the bookstore herself. She loved the contact with the school children early in the morning and with the adults who wandered in during the day. It was a new way for her to connect with people, after losing the Nafaripi people and her babies. There was some sweetness to life again.

MUJIZAT

Nurturing a thriving crop of new churches could have been work enough for Larry and Shirley for some time—along with some building projects and visits to bolster the morale of the Nafaripi at Sumapero. But a new work was germinating, an improbable work, a work to which at one point they would have strenuously objected. The idea was so wild, so preposterous that they had dismissed it after their trip to the Philippines where the idea was born. The timing was wrong then; it was only the Thanksgiving holiday after the accident. But by the time it came to fruition their attitudes had changed, and they were ready.

When Larry, Shirley, and Chip visited Keith and Kathy in the Philippines, some missionary families befriended them and invited them for Thanksgiving dinner. Among them were Dave and Helen Sheats of the Far Eastern Broadcasting Corporation, and Bill and Lil Tinsley with the Jesus People. A radio announcer with the FEBC in Manila had broadcast the Rascher's accident report in installments, so both couples knew the Raschers' story. They had been praying for them and met them with a plan to present. Bill Tinsley brought up the subject as they were seated, satisfied after a Thanksgiving meal.

"Since we heard of your terrible accident, we've been

praying that the Lord would provide you a boat. One that is seaworthy and will reduce the travel risk for missionary families," he said.

Larry's brow furrowed. "No, we're not interested in a boat now. I appreciate your concern, Bill, but we don't really want a boat." His eyes sought Shirley's, wondering what they'd gotten into.

"But does TEAM need a boat in Irian? How would you feel about our praying for a boat for TEAM?"

"Sure," said Larry, feeling uncomfortable, "as long as I won't be sailing it."

Dave Sheats was a naval reserve officer and called Larry a few days later. "You want to do a little sight-seeing at Subic Bay? I have to go there to see about my reserve duty and we can look in the shipyard for a boat."

Subic Bay was the largest U.S. naval base in south-east Asia. Ships were being overhauled at Subic Bay and refitted for duty at Vietnam. Larry was interested in an inside look.

Dave attended to his business and then guided Larry to the ship junkyard. A collection of rotting hulls littered an asphalt lot. Periodically the navy held public auctions on them. Those that didn't sell were destroyed.

"I don't want any of this stuff, Dave," said Larry, walking between rusty landing craft. "What would we want with any of this?" They picked their way over to the few larger wood-hulled boats.

The sergeant in charge of the shipyard approached them and asked what business they had there, since neither was in uniform. Dave explained that they had come to see about his reserve duty, and that Larry's mission in Irian Jaya needed a boat.

The sergeant's manner was cool. "How much money do you fellas have to invest?"

"Well, uh, really nothing," said Dave. "But I thought. . . ."

"Don't you men understand that the U.S. Navy don't

give nothin' to nobody—ever? It'll cost you $20,000 for anything here, then at least another $20,000 to fix it up. I've got things to do. Don't waste my time." The sergeant escorted them straight back to the gate. Before they knew it, they were standing outside.

"Who is he to push us around? The Lord can supply the money and a boat, if He wants to," Larry said to Dave, a twinkle in his eyes. "Let's go back to the car and pray about it."

They did. And they asked the Lord what they should do next. They decided to talk to the chaplain on base.

They told Chaplain Alex Aronis that they were trying to procure a boat for TEAM's use in Irian Jaya. Then, without Larry's knowledge, while Larry visited the men's room, Dave briefly told the chaplain the story of the Raschers' accident.

The following day Dave received a call. The navy was disposing of about fourteen small boats. The navy could not give a boat to an organization or an individual. But he and Larry could choose one they liked and apply to obtain it through the United States Agency for International Development (USAID).

On their return visit to the shipyard, they found the same sergeant smiling and much more helpful. "Just look the place over and choose what you want," he said. As if in a dream, not quite understanding what was happening or how he got into it, Larry chose a UB ship-to-shore boat that was fifty-two feet long and fifteen feet wide. It had been an open-hull boat with benches around the sides to hold about fifty men. He gazed at its barnacle-encrusted hull. *What in the world would he do with it? How could he get it to Irian? What would the field council say?*

Dave searched for the officer in charge of the boat works. When he described what TEAM Irian needed, the officer identified himself as a Christian. He came over to inspect the chosen boat and the three men stood looking, silently.

"Tell you what we'll do," said the officer. "This is my last year in the navy, and I'd like to serve the Lord in some way here before I leave. I'm teaching a class on boat building to Filipinos. The final exam is to build a boat, and we'll use this boat for that project. When the men aren't busy with navy repair work, we'll put in time on your boat. I don't know how long it'll take, but I think you'll be pleased with it when we're done. We'll make you a boat fit for the Lord's work."

The officer took from his pocket a 3 x 5 index card and a pencil and asked Larry to draw what he wanted. Larry took the card and pencil and sketched the perfect missionary boat with a large hold for transporting supplies and an aft cabin with bunks. A wood hull skinned with fiberglass would be best. He turned over the sketch sheepishly. "Would this be too much?"

The following day the Raschers returned to Irian Jaya.

The TEAM Irian field council was skeptical. Where would they keep the thing? It would be the best boat docked in Manokwari Bay! Who would use it? None of them were sailors. How would they pay for the fuel? Who would maintain it?

Between the paperwork involving the USAID application, the complexities of dealing with the port authorities in the Philippines and in Irian Jaya, and the piecemeal way the refurbishing was done, a year passed. Meanwhile, Larry and Shirley were immersed in the changes at hand: moving to Senggo, the fire, moving to Manokwari, opening the bookstore, the evangelistic meetings.

But as they became more settled into life on the north coast, and began to see all the great possibilities before them for ministry, Larry Rascher had the growing conviction that TEAM Irian needed a boat—not just for hauling their families and stuff around, but for ministry.

Three-fifths of the million-plus inhabitants of Irian

Jaya lived in the cities, in the hundreds of villages, and on islands along the coastline. Northwest of Irian Jaya the myriad islands of Indonesia, the earth's fifth most populous country, fanned out between the Pacific and Indian Oceans. Yet most of the missionaries were concentrated among isolated highland tribes. No mission had a boat ministry.

Larry lay awake at night planning and dreaming. "We could take teams of Manokwari church people on the boat to share their testimonies of faith in the coastal villages. Many of our church people are from Biak and Numfoor and long to tell their relatives on those islands about their new faith. The government would pay us to haul rice and supplies to villages at the same time. That would pay for the fuel."

Shirley could tell what was coming. She did not relish the thought of being on the open seas; but she knew they were caught up in something bigger than themselves. If God was orchestrating this, He would enable them to do it. She didn't dwell on the "what if 's;" she simply waited.

The field council agreed to the venture, with Larry in charge of it. But by the time the boat arrived it wasn't the Raschers' boat or TEAM's boat, it was their churches' boat. On it the Christians of the Wosi and Fanindi churches would travel with the news of their new lives to people of other islands and villages. They had seen a model of the boat, and it was fantastic, unbelievable. Bill Tinsley and his crew jokingly called it the Mudcat; they had sailed her down from Manila amid one hardship after another so that what should have been a trip of ten days took two weeks. But the Manokwari Christians would call it *Mujizat,* "Miracle Boat."

Mujizat's eight-cylinder diesel engine made a dragon-like roar heard across the usually quiet Manokwari Bay. One foggy morning before she got the telephone call, Shirley heard it and knew the boat had arrived. A church leader called from the TEAM Irian office in Manokwari. "*Njonya!* There is a boat here that looks like the model of the *Mujizat!!*" He was so excited he could hardly talk. A few minutes later Larry's VW pulled up at the dock to greet Bill Tinsley and his weary crew.

Within an hour the dock and the water around the boat were alive with the curious. Even after a grueling trip and damage to the fiberglass hull, *Mujizat* was beyond Larry's wildest dreams, and certainly beyond the dreams of the nationals.

It had the lines of an old navy liberty boat, but was outfitted like a small yacht. "Lawrence, come look at this!" exclaimed Shirley from the galley, "Melmac dishes and real silverware!"

The decks fore and aft would easily sleep a "team" of twenty church people plus the boat's crew of five. Canvas canopies provided shade. Amidship sat the wheel house. A large cargo hold was under the deck in the front. Down a companionway in back of the wheel-house was the stern cabin with two bunks on each wall and a small galley. The wood hull and decks were skinned with fiberglass. She was outfitted with ropes, compass, a spare prop and shaft, and a scoochie (a fourteen-foot outboard skiff with a small motor for getting to shore).

It was now a craft worth $75,000. And it was a gift. Not so much from the U.S. Navy, or from USAID, as from the Lord. In their excitement too many people tried to board the boat from the same side. As it tipped precariously Larry herded people to the other side.

That morning, Larry and Shirley and the believers of the Manokwari churches dedicated the *Mujizat* with prayer and singing. The fog lifted slowly up the crescent of green mountains, and with it rose the harmonies of hundreds of voices. *Alleluia, Alleluia.* Larry and Shirley wondered at the journeys ahead of them.

NUMFOOR

Chatter ceased aboard the *Mujizat*. The coconut palms and clean sands of the island of Numfoor were in view. High in the sparkler-like tops of some of the palms, boys had climbed after coconuts and saw the big boat coming.

The beautiful isle had a protective armor. A coral reef encircled the northeastern portion of the ten-hundred-square-mile island, changing the water to brilliant green for miles out to sea. Beautiful but deadly, it could rip even a metal boat, much less the wooden *Mujizat*. There was only one chink in the armor. American GI's had blasted a hole in the reef when General MacArthur built a secret airstrip on Numfoor. The rusted wrecks of fighter planes were still visible through the clear waters of lagoons between the reef and the shore.

The *Mujizat* could hope to get through the opening only at high tide. It was always windy on little Numfoor, so the waves were high, and could smash the boat into the reef like a bathtub toy. There was a government-approved captain aboard, but at times like this he had Larry take charge. As so often was the case, Larry trusted the instincts of a national.

Opor, a wiry, little man, stood in the bow holding onto the cable with his right hand, his left hand raised.

His back was to Larry and he studied the shore. Opor was Numfoorese and a new Christian in the Wosi church of Manokwari. He was a faithful worker, quick to do a job without question or complaint. Opor knew to align the boat's bow with the last coconut tree before the row of knarled manggi-manggi roots. He knew that waves came in cycles: five heavy ones, then three light. After the fifth big one, Opor motioned. Larry gunned the motor. All he could see was Opor's left hand, but he knew that was enough. After fourteen hours at sea they were in the quiet waters inside the reef, for the first evangelistic mission of the *Mujizat*.

With the roar of the diesel engine, children came skimming across the water in dugout canoes, whooping and hollering. With three or more to a canoe, they seemed like swarming insects. The *Mujizat* dropped anchor, and they jockeyed for a position alongside her, like a bunch of curious American kids on bikes.

From on board, people called for children to tell relatives they had arrived.

In addition to Larry, TEAM Irian field chairman Ron Hill, and a government-approved crew, it had been hard to select which twenty people to bring. At departure time many more nationals than the boat could hold had crowded the dock in Manokwari with their sleeping mats, pots and small bundles of cloth under their arms. Even after twenty had been taken aboard and the passenger list submitted to the government official, people tried to jump on as the boat pulled away. Sometimes there were fistfights on the docks before they left.

Numfoor was sixty miles due east of Manokwari. Seventy-five miles beyond Numfoor was the larger island of Biak. The Numfoor-Biak peoples were among the most civilized and well-educated in Irian Jaya, thanks to the Dutch. The religion of the islands was a mix of lifeless Christian orthodoxy and cargo cult.

Larry lowered the scoochie, loaded on his motor-cycle, and went to shore. While the team waited on board the *Mujizat,* Larry rode to the police compound to deliver the papers which gave their visit government sanction. American Marines had built a network of wide asphalt roads encircling the island. Now the jungle had devoured all but a slim path of old asphalt along the center where the people walked.

The team could only visit those villages to which they had been invited. This visit, like many to follow, would involve ten days on the island with another day of traveling each way.

The team was shuttled to shore in the scoochie and chores began. Everyone had a job: fishing, cooking in large pots over a fire on the shore, finding a spring or well for their drinking water, washing clothes. Once meet-ings commenced, evening mealtimes became sporadic; they didn't know when their next meal would be— sometimes at midnight—so the team prepared a large midday meal.

Most of the thirty–seven villages of Numfoor were built on stilts along the shore, complete with outhouse holes directly over the sea and high-standing pig pens (although the pigs were also allowed in the houses). The streets were a maze of planks made from sticks and branches. There were fifty or so houses in Bawai, where the *Mujizat* first anchored.

The first night, as the team lounged around the decks of *Mujizat* before succumbing to sleep, a man from Bawai came aboard. He said that a number of Bawai people were eager to greet them and to hear about God. So the next morning they would hold their first meeting.

Larry sat a while on the deck that night. He had come without Shirley the first trip, anxious to see that all went well on the boat before he brought her. There were quiet murmurings—conversations here and there.

The bay was dotted with the lanterns of the men of Bawai spearfishing in their canoes. Larry could see the sparkling phosphorus trails of fish swimming near the *Mujizat*. Someone on deck began singing, and other voices joined in. Then it was quiet again, with a breeze off the sea. How powerful a part the rivers and the sea played in their lives: mighty opponents, life-givers, vital links to unreached peoples. How amazing the workings of the unseen Captain of their lives.

In Bawai the next morning the team joined a dozen families in one of the longer houses. The sleeping mats had been removed from the floor. There were no other furnishings. They entered and sat quietly.

First Larry greeted their hosts while a team member translated into Numfoorese. Then a crew member, from Bawai, slowly stood up and told in Numfoorese how he had recently met Jesus Christ. When he finished, two Bawai women from Manokwari stood and publicly shared their faith with their relatives. Women of Bawai did not speak in public. This was a curious thing to the Bawai people. The message of these women must be important for them to have the courage to stand up and tell it.

As the *Mujizat* was lifting anchor that night to move to another village inside the reef, Bawai people brought food to the boat as a token of appreciation. In Bawai, for the first time, many people were weighing what they had heard about the possibility of knowing Christ personally and being assured of eternal life and release from their fears.

Word of the visitors had traveled through Numfoor, so the next village was ready for them. While the *Mujizat* team saw to their morning chores, villagers gathered benches under the coconut trees. All 200 were waiting after the team had eaten their midday meal. The Hill family had returned from furlough, and the Raschers were now living next-door to them in

Manokwari. Ron Hill spoke to the people about the simple but profound words of John 5:24: *Truly, truly, I say to you, he who hears My word, and believes Him who sent Me, has eternal life, and does not come into judgment, but has passed out of death into life (NAS).*

On the third day Larry and a few helpers went by scoochie to visit a house on a rise behind the village of Andai. Chuck Sweatte and his family, TEAM missionaries, had begun visiting Numfoor from Manokwari, and had built a house there in 1968. The Sweattes had gone home on furlough, with Chuck ill, after a year of evangelism on the island. Chuck's health had prevented their return. "We want you to watch the house," Chuck had said to Benni, a Yemanu villager, when they left. "Keep the grass cut and guard the house. TEAM will send you the *rupiahs*." Benni was still there five years later, living all alone in the separate study Chuck had built out back. The grass had been recently cut. The island police had "sealed" the door and windows of the house with string and sealing wax.

Larry saw the Sweatte house as a place which could be home base on their trips to Numfoor. With a policeman present, he broke the wax seals and string and entered the house, which had been shut up for five years. It was not vacant. Hanging from a rafter was a termite nest, like a huge cocoon. They swept it out the door and set fire to it in the yard. The house was built of ironwood and cement, so the damage was not irreparable. Larry looked through the screened windows of the house to the clean stretch of beach below. Shirley would scrub this place, Larry knew, and make it a fine home.

The next day the team was warmly received at Andai, where there were believers who had not had any teaching since the Sweatte's departure.

Often their meetings were held in the relative cool of the evening. They stretched a sheet between two trees to serve as a movie screen. The team sang, two or three members gave testimonies and a brief message, then they showed a film, in Indonesian, on the life of Christ. Sometimes the team just entered a village to meet the people and get acquainted rather than to preach.

In the years to follow, the *Mujizat* would visit Numfoor several times. Four churches with national pastors arose on Numfoor, not without persecution.

But the mission of the *Mujizat* was twofold. Not only the villagers but the missionaries themselves were learning. Each time a team visited island peoples with the *Mujizat*, which happened roughly four times a year during periods of calmer seas, each team member came home stronger and more encouraged in his or her own faith. Each learned that he or she had spiritual gifts which were valuable to a group of Christians who ate and slept and worked closely together. Sometimes there were storms at sea during the trip. Sometimes factions tried to run them out of a village. They grew in their dependence upon prayer, and in the joy of seeing prayers answers; and they were able to tell others about the richest blessing of their lives.

MANOKWARI

By summer 1974, the Raschers had been in Manokwari two years. Once again they had assembled household goods, with the help of supporters back home—goods for "civilized" north coast living. They now lived next-door to the Hills and continued as church planters, bookstore manager, station hostess, and builder.

There was so much to do—so much more than could be done. There were the high energy demands of working with rapidly growing churches. In addition, Shirley traveled with Larry to building projects, or to preach. When she got back there was constant company, a backlog of correspondence, paperwork for the bookstore, a course in Indonesian to teach to incoming missionaries.

On his way home from delivering building supplies to the hospital at Senggo, Larry took the *Mujizat* to Sumapero. As he began to move his family's remaining furniture and household goods onto the boat, the old women of the village lined up at the front door and wouldn't let him pass. Larry knew they could get violent, so he sought to appease them. He knew the dining table was too large to move. "See," he said, "we are leaving this table and chairs and the beds because we're going to come back."

And they did go back a couple of times a year; but they wouldn't be moving back to Sumapero. Besides the fact that they no longer had the equipment it took to operate on the south coast, they knew they had a work now in Manokwari. They knew, too, that there would be no other missionary family available or willing to live with the Nafaripi, learn their language, and help them. But Jonas would continue to do what he could.

Larry left the table he had built large enough for his family and the TEAM Irian field council. Gone were the good meals, the talk and laughter around the table by lantern light.

It was hard on Shirley to have all three children away in Manila, not even having Chip to visit at the Sentani school. The kids were a solid, happy focal point for Shirley, and it was hard to have them so far away.

The asthma and allergies which Shirley had battled all her years on the field—not letting them keep her down—were a constant drain on her.

That summer Larry was back to building six days a week. Jim Bruursema, a buddy from Michigan, had for two years taken over much of TEAM's building work in Irian Jaya. But Jim and his family had just returned to the States.

Larry's main project, which Jim Bruursema had overseen, was to complete a TEAM guesthouse and a hostel, or dorm, for TEAM children at the school at Sentani. The hostel was to be dedicated as the Rascher Children Memorial Hostel in memory of Karen and Greg. It was completed in the summer of 1974, just after Chip graduated from the Sentani school and just in time for the next school term. No Rascher children would ever live in the new hostel, but Chip had his share of fun playing around the construction site.

At Faith Academy the kids kept busy and happy. Kathy was social secretary on student council and planned all the school social events: a welcome party, a Hawaiian luau, a progressive dinner where the students traveled from dorm to dorm for the meal courses aboard a bus decorated to look like an airplane (complete with stewardesses, a pilot, and "passport" tickets). As a student, as social planner, as a dorm friend, Kathy was a girl who could be counted on.

Faith Academy was strong in academics, sports, and social and spiritual growth opportunities. It also provided a little polish for children who had grown up on a primitive field. The staff understood kids like Keith and Chip Rascher. They helped them settle into high school while trying not to squelch the enthusiasm and drive that was part of what made good missionaries.

Meanwhile, Larry was a popular conference speaker. He was known as a good preacher who related well with the people. He and Shirley were fluent in Indonesian, and the government was on a push to have all nationals taught to speak Indonesian.

Three times they led conferences for Christian and Missionary Alliance missionaries Tom and Fran Bozeman in the Grand Valley of the Baliem River, in the interior highlands among the huge Dani tribe. In the past few years thousands of Danis had burned their fetishes and had turned to the living God. They were hungry to be taught. Tom Bozeman was a tall man with plenty of enthusiasm and big ideas.

"Within my eyesight," said Tom Bozeman, standing with Larry on his front porch in the Baliem Valley, "are 17,000 Dani believers." No white man had laid eyes on this majestic valley until the twentieth century. But the Dani tribe had lived there for thousands of years, in the grass houses which now dotted the valley below like clusters of giant mushrooms.

The first time Larry and Shirley visited the Bozemans was soon after the boating accident. They had spoken to Dani Bible school students and their wives. During this second visit in the fall of 1974, Larry preached twenty-eight times in ten days, both at the Bible school and in churches within the Baliem Valley.

Danis are great storytellers. Before they became Christians, the men sat around and talked while the women gardened. Though many of them were now Christians, they continued the same basic practice. If they could find a Christian man who was an interesting speaker, they listened to him all day.

Larry gave illustrations to which the nationals could relate. He dramatized everything: running, jumping up to sit on the table, lying on the floor. What a challenge this made for Obed, the Dani Bible school graduate who served as Larry's interpreter.

Obed was blind in one eye. He was scrupulously accurate in translating each word and imitating each gesture. One evening Larry came forward from the podium to make a point. He thrust out one arm, barely missing a wooden post. Obed came up from behind Larry and socked the post on his blind side. "Careful Rascher," Tom Bozeman's voice boomed from the back of the room. "You're going to hurt my man!"

MAF pilots took Larry and Tom up the valley to remote churches. The night before a flight, they prayed with the pilot for an outpouring of the Holy Spirit the next day. They had deep assurance that the Lord was going to do something special, and they were not disappointed. There was revival in the Baliem Valley. After each meeting many Danis stood to indicate a commitment to a life of obedience to Jesus Christ. In the Dani meetings former savages prayed aloud fervently, openly confessing their sins and determining to follow the Lord wholeheartedly.

One day they were up early and in the Cessna for the seven-minute flight to a church up the valley. By 7:00 a.m. there were nearly a thousand Danis sitting on the dirt floor of the church, with as many outside.

There were no benches, no pulpit. "Tom, where do you preach from?" Larry asked. The room was thick with flies, heat and dark, sweaty bodies.

"Just work your way to the middle and they'll spread out a little," he replied.

"How long shall I go?"

"Just go till you're done."

By 10:00 a.m. Larry was mighty thirsty. "Can I take a break?" he called back to Tom.

"Sure."

Dani pastors stood up as Larry left the room. They led the people in Dani songs. Some people rose and gave testimonies. Some quoted Scripture.

"How much longer should I go?" Larry asked Tom as they returned.

"Just go till you're done. Say 'Amen' when you're finished."

At noon Larry again looked at his friend. Even Larry was played out. "Hey, Bozeman, is there anything to eat around here?"

They went to the pastor's grass home where a whole pig had been roasted for the two missionaries.

Meanwhile, in and around the church Dani women took sweet potatoes from the net bags they carried around their foreheads and hanging down their backs. They ate. Babies nursed. Men talked.

These mountain people were smaller than coastal natives. They had strong legs from traveling fast in the mountains on foot. The women were plump and healthy. Some Danis wore clothes. Otherwise the men wore only a gourd and the women grass skirts.

When Larry and Tom returned from the meal, it looked as though no one had moved. Larry kidded a Dani on his endurance of Larry's preaching. "*Bapak*, I was ten hours getting here. I walked all night. I swam the Baliem River. I would have been very disappointed if you didn't preach long," he said.

Larry began again, encouraged, and preached till the plane came in the late afternoon.

For the final two days, open meetings were held in a field near Pyramid. Six thousand Danis sat to listen to *Bapak Pendita* Rascher. While standing in the middle near Larry, Obed translated, shouting out in Dani. Interpreters standing farther out caught the message and relayed it. The Danis could understand perhaps half the Indonesian. But interpreters were used so that nothing would be missed.

Two years later Larry and Shirley would again come at the Bozeman's invitation—this time to Wamena, where the Bozemans relocated the Dani Bible school.

Three Dani couples came up to Larry after a meeting. "What are they here for, Tom?" Larry asked.

"They say they are Bible school students and they are barren and want children. They want you to pray for them."

Larry prayed, but with inner struggle and without conviction. How did he know these three couples were meant to have children? Yet Larry had been learning that often while he might do the praying, the people did the believing: simple, straightforward belief.

A year later Larry was en route through Wamena, with the Cessna revving its engines, when a couple came running up the center of the airstrip toward the plane. They had to show their baby to *Bapak* Rascher, and thank him for praying. What of the other two couples? He never saw them again.

Eventually the Bozemans were given oversight of the outstation of Silimo, a half-hour flight up the valley from Wamena. When Tom and Fran first visited there, they found two Bible school graduates had come to work among that tribe. The men told the Bozemans that they were never going home to their own people: "When *Tuan* Rascher came and talked to us soon after losing his children, he stayed on in Irian. We're not going home either." With a special Christmas offering they had received, the Bozemans paid for the men and their families to be flown to visit their home in the Ilaga Valley for two weeks. It had been a hardship on their wives, particularly, not to see their families for so long.

In the fall, Larry and Shirley flew to Sumapero for a week. The people were in desperate need of medical help. They saw cases of hepatitis, pneumonia, and meningitis. Shirley immediately went to work treating thirty to fifty natives a day, with the help of Dr. Dresser via shortwave radio.

Jonas, the capable teacher/evangelist, was growing discouraged with eighty-five students in six grades. The Rascher house was riddled with termites. The airstrip was badly overgrown with weeds. It was hard to leave the village like this, with a furlough year approaching. They yearned to see a family living and working among the Nafaripi.

At Christmas the kids came home from Manila for two-and-a-half weeks. There were good times in the house on the hill in Manokwari.

Larry and Shirley stayed up late the first night, getting a three-way account of life at Faith Academy from their "dorm refugees." How Chip had grown!

Keith and Chip were merciless teases. Kathy was usually the brunt of their jokes. They couldn't help it; she was so nice. They liked to imitate Dad, too, especially at the table. As the boys said, Larry was from the "Good Old Dad" school, and sat enthroned at the head of the table. Larry had only to look at an item and Shirley would get it or pass it to him. Also, Larry had a tendency to get to talking and carry a bit of his food on his chin.

Kathy's bedroom had been added on the back of the house and was entered through the boys' bedroom. She was sure rats lived in the walls, and Kathy didn't like snakes, bugs or rats.

At night Kathy laid awake with the sheet pulled up to her eyes, watching. There was a hole in the wall a few inches above the side of her bed. She knew the rats came from there. She saw four in her room one night, their eyes glistening. She watched them all night. One ran over her bed. That was enough!

No one believed Kathy about the rats, but the next night she settled in to sleep on the living-room sofa. The living room was softly bright with moonlight. The house was quiet, but for the tree frogs and murmuring insects beyond the screens. Kathy laid awake, this time unafraid, enjoying being at home.

A piercing scream brought the family to the living room. Kathy had flipped on the lights and fled to the kitchen. A snake, lounging along the window frame, was now gliding down the drapes.

The family roared with laughter. Larry disposed of the snake, which the boys thought wasn't big enough for a fuss. Kathy shut herself and the cat in her bedroom for the night, and took her chances with the rats.

Later that night when the rest of the family was asleep, Keith and Chip ever so slowly and quietly opened Kathy's door—they spent ten minutes just getting it open. On hands and knees they crawled into her room and rolled balled-up dark socks over her bed and along the floor. They stealthily fetched and rolled them again and again until they aroused their sleeping sister. She fell for the trick the first time. Later she wised up and the boys lost interest.

In Manokwari the boys spent most of their vacation water-skiing in the bay, or repairing the outboard motor so they could go water-skiing. For their Christmas present the boys could count on a fifty-five-gallon drum of fuel from Mom and Dad. Sometimes they connived a second drum, scraping barnacles and painting the *Mujizat* to pay for it.

Nationals skied with them, especially a little short

fellow with a deep voice whom the boys carried on their shoulders when they skied. Phil Hill next door didn't like to ski; however, the boys persuaded Phil that he was a great boat driver so that he would pull them.

They skied early in the morning, while the bay was smooth, and were home in time for breakfast. The children from town would be ready and waiting on the town pier for the *tuans*, who had zinc oxide dabbed on their fair noses. The kids lined up on the pier, and Keith and Chip took turns slaloming past them, spraying them with wide rooster-tails. The native children howled with glee.

Further into the bay the skiers sprayed and nearly capsized fishermen in dugout canoes. Sometimes a fisherman dove into the water before the boat swerved, thinking it would hit him. Some fishermen waved them over, eager to cool off. Others stood drenched in their canoes, shaking their fists and swearing at the boys; these the boys learned to avoid.

Kathy liked to water-ski, except for the fact that it put her at the mercy of whichever brother was pulling her. They were liable to make her fall in front of a tourist boat or keep pulling her when she wanted to go in.

When Phil wasn't around and the boys were hard up for a driver, they used Kathy. One day when she was pulling Chip he motioned for her to go around into the next bay. Children playing on the beach swam toward them as the boat approached. Although they were still quite a distance from the boat, the children in the water frightened Kathy. What if she ran over one of them? She wanted to stop, go the other way, do something quickly, but Chip was on the back. She panicked and pulled the Evinrude motor out of gear while it was open full throttle. Chip sank in the water as the motor gave a sickening whine. She had sheared a pin. Once again the boat was laid up. Kathy helped Shirley in the bookstore.

When the wind rose on the ocean later in the day, Keith and Chip surfed or dove along the coral reef. They dove freestyle with masks, snorkels and fins, and earned reputations even among the nationals as good divers. Chip's record was a depth of sixty-seven feet, and Keith eventually matched it. Americans didn't believe them, but it was true. They dove to spearfish, or sometimes to gather coral for a coral garden they made for Shirley. They always took nationals with them. The boys loved the ocean, but had a healthy respect for its dangers, particularly waves and strong currents.

Not all missionary children enjoyed life on the field as much as did these. Not all parents let their children mingle so freely with the nationals or dive or spearfish or go off into the jungle to hunt. Some missionary kids went home on school vacations to read books. Just as in the States, on the mission field in Irian Jaya some parents were more protective of their children. Larry and Shirley did sometimes worry about the boys' adventures. But when it came down to it they respected the boys' good judgment and knew they were mature beyond their years.

Larry and Shirley were constantly with nationals— working, talking, playing—and the children followed suit. Consequently a mutual love grew with the Indonesian people, particularly the Irianese.

Even the native animals had a place in their hearts. The favorite pet in the Rascher household was Chip's parrot, Popeye. Chip found Popeye in a nest which had fallen to the ground. Popeye had a wide vocabulary, whistled *Silent Night,* and sang with the radio. In Sumapero he flew after their boat when they traveled up-river. They nearly lost Popeye one day when he hopped from Shirley's head to the moving wringer of the washing machine.

Freddie and Freda were small, brown, tree kangaroos

which had been sold to the Raschers by nationals. They lived in a huge cage Larry and the boys built in the backyard. Freda spent much of her time up in a guava tree just outside the cage. Chip sat in the tree with Freda and ate guavas. When Freddie and Freda were allowed in the house, they slid comically on the slick concrete floors.

New Year's Eve in Manokwari was celebrated with a motorcycle parade at midnight. Hundreds of motor-cycles turned out—all there were in the town. The object was to be the head motorcycle in the parade, just behind the lead truck. A secondary objective was to be in front of Keith and Chip Rascher. That meant burst-ing to the front, then slowing down behind the truck, then lurching to the front again as many other motor-cycles attempted the same thing. Chip rode the family motorcycle, a 185. Keith borrowed the Hill's 100. After the parade, just because it was New Year's Eve, the boys water-skied in the bay with a spotlight rigged up on the front of the boat, and Phil (a good sport) driving.

Fortunately for Shirley, after the kids returned to Manila their beds were empty only two days before the beginning of a second round of city-wide evangelistic meetings in Manokwari. Once again there were many new believers to be fed in the Word and shepherded by the Manokwari churches. The spring sped by. Larry and Shirley flew to Kathy and Keith's high school graduation ceremonies in Manila.

The commencement was traumatic for each of the graduates, who had lived and studied and played together and would be parting to go literally to the ends of the earth. The graduates sobbed and clung to each other, including Keith and his buddies. The following day the Rascher family left for another furlough year in the States. After furlough, Kathy and Keith would stay in the States for work and college, leaving home life in Indonesia.

States. After furlough, Kathy and Keith would stay in the States for work and college, leaving home life in Indonesia.

When the family left Manokwari for furlough, the *Mujizat* sat at the pier in Manokwari Bay where it collected barnacles. There was no one else with the time, interest, or the ability to take her helm.

The peanut grinder, purchased with high hopes the furlough before, had never reached its intended home in Sumapero. Young missionary Craig Preston, to Larry's delight, had taken on the project. But it never provided much income because the students had to buy their peanuts in the market. It would have been ideal if the students had been able to grow their own peanuts; but it was too much ordeal to set up and clean the grinder for one sack. It did make good peanut butter, though. The peanuts were cooked in hot sand in two huge woks over an open fire. Eventually it rusted beyond repair, and Larry wished he had sold it to a Chinese merchant.

In its lifetime the peanut grinder produced one small batch of peanut butter at the Bible school in Saowi for the students to sell. The peanut roaster, meanwhile, was roasting French fries for happy students at the boarding school in Sentani.

The ten-horse Kohler motor Larry had rigged up for the peanut grinder served a stint at the TEAM sawmill in Agats on the south coast when the planer motor broke down. Then Larry lost track of it. Missionaries tended to share goods around to the point that the original owner could easily lose track of an object.

The Raschers had moved Moses to Manokwari, where the family hoped to be of help to him. They would always feel bound up with Moses, responsible for him somehow, deeply grateful for his part with the children in the accident. And Moses felt part of their family and that he belonged with them.

Having completed only the first six grades, Moses was not qualified for a government subsidy as a teacher. For a while he lived in a house behind the bookstore as a night watchman. He was a main worker on the *Mujizat;* but other team members, Biakers from the Wosi church, looked down on him because he was from a more primitive tribe and didn't speak their language. He attended church occasionally, but never fit in. Larry wanted to spend time with Moses to disciple him consistently, but with Larry's travel and other responsibilities, he could manage it only sporadically.

Eventually Moses left Manokwari. During the Raschers' furlough he took a wife from a tribe considered lower than his own. She was not a believer and brought him trouble. Larry and Shirley wished that instead of trying to improve Moses' lot, they had left him to fend for himself in Kokonao.

PART THREE

NEVER GOODBYE

JOURNEY TO NUMFOOR

On furlough Chip attended tenth grade in Hudsonville, Michigan. Kathy candled eggs on an egg farm for a year to earn money to attend Columbia Bible College.

For Keith, life in America was an uncomfortable fit. In the summer he played soccer. He also umpired night-time softball games, until the recreation department figured out he didn't know much about the sport. He had planned to start college in the fall until he found he had the chance to play soccer for the Chicago Sting. The day he was to sign a contract, Keith hurt his knee. After his knee surgery, he was too late to get into college that year. So Keith, also, spent the year in Michigan, sorting, bagging and loading potatoes.

After that furlough, when Larry, Shirley and Chip returned to Irian Jaya in the spring of 1976, Kathy was entering Columbia Bible College. Keith was starting Liberty Bible College on a soccer scholarship. Both were living for the summer with Ken and Judy Logan, who provided a loving home-away-from-home. The Logans even had a ski boat and lived on a lake.

Shirley thought as long as Kathy and Keith were well provided for, they would be fine and so would she. So why could she not quit crying on the flight out of St. Louis? And why were they crying at the airport?

She found that the very thought that she would not see them for four years was almost more than she could bear.

Shirley and Larry heard in Irian Jaya later in the summer that another knee injury meant more surgery for Keith, and no soccer that year—and no soccer scholarship. That fall three months passed without a letter from Keith. Kathy did not see him often and didn't know much; but she was concerned about him.

The loss of soccer was a blow to Keith. But beyond that, for the first time in his life, he felt a misfit. He wasn't used to the hypocrisy he saw around him. Students whom he knew lived a double standard were upheld as paragons of Christian virtue.

Keith had to figure out for himself if the Christian life was really all it was supposed to be. He experimented briefly with conduct he'd been taught was not right, but he decided that was not the way to happiness.

At Christmas break in 1977—Chip's last break before he, too, finished at Faith Academy and left for the States—the family drew back together after a year-and-a-half apart. Kathy and Keith flew to Irian Jaya from Michigan—Keith with his disillusionment. Chip came from Manila.

There were long, leisurely family dinners on the hill in Manokwari. The boys used their drum of fuel water-skiing in the bay.

Larry and Shirley asked the kids if they thought it would be a good idea for them to come to the States for an extended furlough when Chip graduated, so they could be together there for some of their college years. Each of the children replied yes.

If Keith was any different when he arrived, Larry and Shirley didn't notice it. They were so happy to have him with them that they didn't pry or scrutinize.

Keith had left school with no intention of returning for the spring semester. He had in mind lying on the beach, sifting his problems in the sand. Larry had another idea. "If you'll give me your mornings, Son, you can do what you want in the afternoons."

So Keith helped Larry measure and frame the rafters for the Wosi church. He refiberglassed the *Mujizat*. He taught Sunday school classes with Kathy at the Wosi church. He was a big help to Larry, and Larry saw his son becoming a man.

Keith had always felt totally at home with the Irianese. But now he saw something new happening. It occurred to him that the Lord was using him—Keith Rascher—to serve these people. He had not grown up with any particular realization that the Lord was using his parents, but he now saw that as well.

Kathy was also realizing new things this visit; but one discovery wasn't a happy one. When Keith and Chip sought Moses out and brought him over, Kathy, particularly, was shocked to see him. Moses had taken up his own life and had distanced himself from the Raschers. He no longer looked like a big brother to Kathy, but a burdened, much older man.

Chip returned to Faith Academy, where he was student body president, soon after Christmas. Kathy and Keith joined their parents and new TEAM missionaries Hemerde and Phyllis Thomas on an evangelistic trip to Numfoor aboard the *Mujizat*. They all looked forward to sharing the adventure. Kathy also anticipated returning to college with a tan.

They planned the trip, got the necessary government permissions, chose the crew and the team of Wosi church believers who would be aboard, and waited through four days of rain.

When the weather cleared Larry got all aboard and the motor running. They left at midnight, weaving through the twinkling lights of fishermen in the bay.

The *Mujizat*, a functional and by no means elegant craft, was by its size the Princess of Manokwari Bay. Another boat left for Numfoor alongside her that night.

It was a much more typical boat, perhaps twelve feet long, with an outboard motor and tiny open-sided cabin. At least thirty people were packed aboard (plus assorted animals), standing or sitting, hanging onto anything to keep from pitching into the water. The water line was perhaps six inches below the deck. The people waved and called to the *Mujizat*, as if it held celebrities. "That is crazy," the *tuans* aboard the *Mujizat* agreed. However, they understood that Biakers were master mariners, who knew a way, for example, to use balancing beams of light wood, running front to back underneath the boat, to keep it from tipping over.

Exhausted from the preparations, Larry laid down on a bunk in the tiny aft cabin. The cabin was eight feet wide with two bunks against the walls on either side of a narrow walkway. Kathy, Phyllis Thomas and Shirley were asleep in the other bunks.

As soon as they got out to sea Larry awakened with a queasy stomach and a racing heart. It was raining again—hard—and the sea was rough. "No, Lord. Why this time with Shirley aboard?" He lay on his bunk listening and praying, wishing that he wasn't hearing what he was. It wasn't just Shirley, although heaven knew that that was enough. Keith and Kathy, the Thomases, the Wosi church people. There were many souls aboard and he felt responsible for them.

At about 2:00 a.m. Opor came for Larry, who slipped on his rubber thongs and quietly stole from the rolling room. Larry's face was white. He knew why the captain had sent for him. The captain would not be responsible in such a storm when the owner was on board, a *tuan* who was a sailor, he assumed, and would know what was to be done.

The night was completely greenish black—the sky, the walls of huge waves. Larry pulled his way to the pilot house by whatever he could grasp. Water scoured the deck with each wave.

Larry took the wheel. The pilot house was jammed with people finding shelter. The Wosi people were stoic when afraid. They silently gave Larry room. Keith was there, too, and Hemerde. The waves were long, rolling ten to fifteen feet high.

The *Mujizat's* wheel was perhaps two feet across. Larry braced himself with his feet wide apart. He grabbed the railing under the window with his left hand and spun the wheel with his right. To hold the boat to meeting the waves at just the right angle meant he had to continually overcompensate, spinning the big wheel, the sea being more powerful than the small rudder. He had to spin the wheel at the precise moment so the boat would roll across the wave instead of being caught sideways and capsized in it.

Between waves, in the troughs, the *Mujizat* was in a watery pit. As the boat turned and met each new wave, water pounded the decks, front to back.

A woman from the Wosi church, a cook on the *Mujizat's* journeys, watched silently from the back corner. She was scared, and she was not by nature a fearful woman, nor were her people a fearful people. She watched the *Bapak Pendita* silently. As long as he was steering, she knew they would be all right.

Keith stood in the darkness for a long time watching his dad before he spoke. He could feel that his father was again on the Ebenezer. He felt strangely outside the combat in which his father was engaged.

"Let me take it, Dad," Keith said at length, as Larry groaned with the strength it took to steer against the tumult.

Larry gave the wheel reluctantly. For a quarter of an hour, perhaps, Keith held the boat. But by then he was so played out that he didn't trust his own strength, and had to give it back. He knew he was as strong as his dad; but there was something missing. He couldn't do it—some fiber was missing, some spirit of fight. He was in awe of the strength and endurance the fight took. Could Dad withstand it? "If you get us through this, Lord, I'll serve you," Keith prayed. "I'll go to Moody and I'll go to the mission field and I'll serve you however you want. Please get us through this." God only knew what his mom must be thinking.

Hemerde knew that Larry didn't have the strength to do what was required. If they got to Numfoor, it would be the Lord's doing.

Shirley was sitting on her bunk with the many women who had wedged into the aft cabin to squat or sit. Shirley had taken treasures out of her purse—passports, photos, her wedding and mother's rings, her glasses, her medications, all things she had lost on the Ebenezer—and tucked them into the fabric cover of a flotation device which she clutched to her breast. She thought of the tooth of a sawtooth fish she'd lost before, too. It was a symbol Keith had given her and Larry when he became a Christian at age four.

She thought of what else she had lost on the Ebenezer. She knew they were going over and was ready to jump at any time.

Kathy watched her mother, and felt with her the horror of the wreck of the Ebenezer. Shirley told her quietly it reminded her of that.

Phyllis was praying the Lord would spare her and Hemerde for the sake of their two children. Shirley thought this would be the end, and Phyllis thought this would be the end. Kathy was too young to know.

Prayers went up from all over the boat. Dark hours passed.

Sometimes Opor spelled Larry. Opor, a wiry national, could hold onto the boat with one hand and lift a twenty-four-cell truck battery with the other. But Opor, too, did not have the endurance to fight Larry's fight.

At daylight the sea was no calmer; but the sense of helplessness had gone which thrives in darkness and shadows. Numfoor was not in sight. The sea was slate grey, still swollen and angry. The rain continued.

Finally they saw the beacon light on Numfoor, and around 9:00 a.m. they brought the *Mujizat* along the back, more sheltered side of the island and through the coral reef to haven at the village of Saribi. Swells of relief and prayers of gratitude ascended from the boat. Keith dove off the boat and spearfished.

The team got to shore as quickly as possible and enjoyed a breakfast of rice, koladi and fish cooked in banana leaves. They enjoyed some unexpected entertainment: the other boat which had left Manokwari with them came bobbing into the harbor. All its drenched but rejoicing passengers waved and called once again. It was impossible! But there they were.

After a meeting in Saribi, when the *Mujizat* raised anchor to proceed to the next village, they found that both the propeller and the bolt which held it had fallen off. Divers recovered the propellor in the sand below, but not the bolt. It occurred to Larry that only the constant motion of the boat in the storm had held the propellor in place without the bolt. Otherwise they would have been adrift, the propeller lost in deep water. Again there were prayers of praise.

Larry called by radio for an MAF flight. Shirley and Phyllis flew back to Manokwari. Shirley was ill, and neither of them wanted to face a sea journey home. Larry joined them to get the spare shaft from his *gudang* in Manokwari and take it to the shipyard to have a bolt made to fit. Meanwhile the boat team awaited Larry's return.

Keith's jobs on the boat team included spearfishing for food, transporting the team and equipment from ship to shore, and setting up projectors. He felt part of something significant. He felt his long love of the Irianese was rekindled.

Although the open-air meetings were hindered by

rain three days during this stay in Numfoor, the team was able to visit some new villages and met generally encouraging response. But as usual they found that the ministry of the *Mujizat* put them into battle with the island's religious establishment, and into battle with the forces of the air which did not want to see Numforeese brought to faith in Jesus Christ. Often in villages where some families wanted them to come, others grumbled and opposed them. The Numfooreese were a hot-tempered people. Invariable, though, they found that following a display of opposition, more villagers came to Christ. It was as if the villagers thought, "If these people can stand up to us, there must be something in it."

In the village of Bawai a cargo cult had infiltrated the village Dutch Reformed church. Eleven men had been beaten by the local policeman in Bawai, in front of their wives, because of their stand for Jesus Christ.

The last meeting was held in the village of Yemburuo, outside the home of Wambrau. Wambrau was not a tall man, but barrel-chested. His legs were bowed and covered with sores. At sixty he was still diving, deep, for five, six, or seven minutes, any day that there was neither wind nor high waves. Wambrau hunted purple oyster-like shells which he sold to Chinese, who made a delicacy of the soft insides. His feet were like wide fins. And his hearing was nearly gone from diving so deep.

Wambrau had long been a leader on Numfoor. Before World War II he was trained and employed by the Dutch Reformed Church, the GKI, as a school teacher and pastor at Yemburuo. He fortified himself with alcohol on Sunday mornings for the courage and inspiration to face his congregation.

When the Japanese occupied Numfoor, they looked to Wambrau to make the villagers work. If they didn't, Wambrau was beaten.

When the American GI's took Numfoor, and built an airstrip near Yemburuo, Wambrau one day found many American dollars in a wallet under a tree. Wambrau hid the treasure, saving it for the soldier who had lost it. The GI who later returned looking was tall and black, handsome in his uniform. If natives of Irian Jaya had one lingering memory of the days Americans lived on their islands, it is of the fact that blacks served alongside whites and were treated as equals.

As time passed Wambrau had trouble with the GKI over his pension, which seldom came. When TEAM missionary Chuck Sweatte built a home near Yemburuo in 1969, Wambrau listened to the man and was impressed with his message. He threatened to change to the TEAM church if the GKI did not come forth with his wages.

When Larry first brought the *Mujizat* to Numfoor in 1972, Wambrau stood in the back, listening, and the Lord seemed to be speaking to him. Again his pension was withheld and he told the GKI, "That's it. I'm going to listen to those people until I understand what they're saying."

On the *Mujizat's* next visit, Larry and the boat team were invited into Wambrau's home. Several village leaders were invited to listen.

By this trip, Wambrau was a leader in his church, understanding plainly that Jesus Christ loved him and had died for him. Tears came to his eyes easily whenever he reminded Larry, or anyone else, that if he had not heard the gospel, he was going to hell.

The *Mujizat* team always used the Sweatte house as a base of operations when at the northern end of the island. And each morning when they were there Ibu Wambrau, *Bapak* Wambrau's grandmotherly wife, walked the two miles from their home to the Sweatte house with a loaf of home-baked bread.

This night, the team showed a movie on the life of

Jesus in front of Wambrau's house. They planned to follow the film with testimonies and singing and a brief message by Larry.

The head of the local GKI church told the team to leave, but the village people wanted to watch this rare entertainment, and remained seated on the ground. The usual sheet had been hung between palms for a screen. More village families were watching and/or listening from their huts.

A drunken villager stood in front of the screen and yelled at the team to leave. He circled in back of it, yanked the speaker chords from the generator and tore down the screen. "Get out of here and leave us alone!" he growled.

From out of the darkness sticks and rocks and any debris at hand were pelted onto the audience. The team quickly gathered the audio-visual equipment and stored it in the home of Wambrau, whose house was bombarded with trash.

Larry spoke calmly to the team. "Don't fight back! Let's go." Larry set a steady, unhurried pace and led the team toward the Sweatte house at nearby Andai. They were followed by hecklers, still throwing whatever was at hand. Some objects hit their marks with a painful thud, but there were no serious injuries. As they walked, the Wosi people formed a protective circle around Larry, Kathy, Keith and Hemerde Thomas. Women sang as they walked the dark path.

The journey home on the *Mujizat* this time was one of the calmest Larry could remember.

Many of the evangelistic trips were rough, but none before or after was as bad as that one. Danger had stalked them so often in Irian Jaya. In the midst of each peril God was with them, as profoundly and certainly as anything else they knew to be true. And with the very fact of that comfort, Larry and Shirley could in turn comfort others, no matter the circumstance.

And if Christ could leave heaven to walk the path of human trials, betrayal, and death on earth, could they not risk some dangers here to tell the Irianese about him? Someone had to run the race, to tell the true story.

As they flew over the Atlantic, U.S. bound, Larry and Shirley saw that the race was worth the price they paid. Theirs was an easy yoke, and it would bring them back.

TROUBLE AT SUMAPERO

On a steamy day early in 1978, two Indonesian officials flew over Manokwari on their way to the island of Biak. There were a handful of passengers in the twin engine Meripati, and a vocal load of chickens in cages jammed in the back.

As they circled over a village near the Manokwari airstrip, one roof stuck out among the checkered squares of corrugated aluminum or zinc or palm leaves. It was hexagonal. Two sections were enclosed. The other four sections were only framed in. People stood on the rafters and walked along them like ants on picnic silverware.

"What is that building there?" asked the official from Biak with some interest.

"The new church in the village of Wosi. It is nearly finished now after only a year."

"Ha! That church down the road is not finished yet and it was started seven years ago. What is the difference with this church? Are the workers being paid by the American mission?"

"No, *Bapak*, no one is paid. The Wosi church people helped build the airstrip at Saowi to raise money. I have seen them take their canoes down the coast and collect black coral in burlap bags, or gravel from the streams for the cement floor and for the blocks for the walls. The women bring in bags of dirt for the floor."

"Come now, my friend. We both know these Irianese do not work day after day in the heat after their regular jobs. They know that work will wait until tomorrow. They will work hard, I admit. But first they have to talk about the job a few days, then they have to rest a few days afterward. But to keep at it like this?"

"It's the *tuan* missionary, *Bapak* Rascher. He drives a truck into the village of Wosi, they say, every day at about 3:00 p.m., after the workers have finished working and had something to eat. He goes in and out of the houses calling for workers."

"And they go with him?"

"As you see. Not every day this many, but always at least a few."

"Isn't that the missionary who brings a big boat of natives to Numfoor?"

"Yes. These people of the Wosi church, there are hundreds of them now. And they are lit by a fire. I have not before seen such a thing," said the official from Manokwari, as they flew over an azure sea, with patches of green where coral bulged near the surface.

In the midst of the building of the Wosi church, Larry Rascher had other work to do. The preceeding summer he had left the Wosi people with work assignments on the church building and had taken Shirley and Chip to Sumapero to visit.

At Sumapero, Chip was astounded to find old playmates married, some with children. For their part, many of his friends had trouble believing that this grown young man before them was Chip, and not Keith.

Chip liked to hang out in the evenings at the home of Jonas, the national teacher and evangelist. Wiry little Jonas had finally taken a wife, Johana, from his tribe on Biak. She was capable and lovely and banished the loneliness of this forsaken place.

Jonas also had a faithful helper, Nimrod, who had

taught at the village of Amar, and Nimrod's wife Fitalia. They brought with them to Sumapero a niece, about seven years old, whom they were raising.

Many of the village boys gathered at Jonas' house to tell stories in the evening. For many years Jonas had lived single in Sumapero and his door was always open. Johana didn't seem to mind. The boys knew Jonas stayed in Sumapero because he loved them and he loved the Lord, and he wasn't trying to get anything from them. Nimrod dropped in, too, sitting in the shadows. He was small and thin and by nature quieter than Jonas. His wife Fitalia was large and strong.

Shirley was occupied just maintaining a household in a primitive setting without a house helper. She scrubbed the place on her hands and knees. She washed the bed frames and all the bedding. She didn't mind managing on the few household goods they still had there: a one-burner stove, a couple of pots and pans. This was still home, where everyone met you at the river when you arrived and saw you off at the river when you departed. In Manokwari a handful of missionaries collaborated in the work. In Sumapero the work, humanly speaking, had been their own.

Larry held meetings in the church Jonas and the Nafaripi had built. Sumeriko, Esapa's son, was now chief and called the people to the meetings with his bamboo horn. Sumeriko had been their houseboy for a while in Sumapero, and for a while in Kokonao, although homesick for his own village. He was easy-going and happy, rather small in stature, but unquestionably capable. He had been a leader both in the church and in the village alongside his father Esapa.

There were other people, new people, lurking on the outskirts of village activity. One of them Larry and Shirley knew: Paulus, a mountain native who had come down and lived with two other mountain boys in the Raschers' *gudang* at Kokonao and had gone to their school. "Lawrence, why is Paulus here? And why is he acting so funny to me?" Shirley asked. But they were too busy reconnecting with their old Nafaripi friends to pursue it.

Soon after returning to Manokwari, Shirley received a phone call from Jonas' relatives in Biak. "We heard Jonas has been killed." The voice was distraught.

"No, no. We just came from Sumapero and we were with Jonas and Johana. They're fine!"

Still, Shirley was alarmed enough to contact Sumapero during the MAF radio SKED the next day. From 8:00 to 8:30 a.m. TEAM Irian's stations logged in and relayed messages.

"We are fine, *Nyona*," Jonas said. "Johana has just had her baby and guess what we have named him? Chip Rascher Faidiban! Um. . . and some people want to join us, *Nyona*. We don't yet know what we will do."

Larry was apprehensive about this cryptic news, remembering the strange faces always on the periphery at Sumapero.

Word came soon after of unrest in the area of Sumapero. A band of disgruntled natives was making the area unsafe for Jonas and Nimrod, government-employed teachers, and they fled with their families to an Asmat village. Newborn Chipper Rascher Faidiban became sick and died in the jungle in flight.

The Indonesian government closed the region of Sumapero while they tried to reestablish peace. Larry and Shirley prayed and waited for the occasional news they got from Jonas, who hoped to return to Sumapero.

In Manokwari their work proceeded on the Wosi church, in the bookstore, with a youth ministry they'd undertaken with Hemerde and Phyllis Thomas, and with Larry's assignment as director of evangelism for TEAM Irian.

One day the military commander from Manokwari, a man Larry knew and trusted, came to Larry at the

TEAM Irian office in Manokwari. "As you know, my jurisdiction includes the Fak Fak past which has authority over the area near where you used to live," he said. "There is no longer a threat from outsiders in the area, and we want the Nafaripi to return to their village. If they return to their old ways in the jungle there will be tribal warfare and trouble. We want you to come with us and tell the Nafaripi to go back to Sumapero."

Larry had no reason, from past dealings, to distrust his friend the commander. And he feared for the Nafaripi in the jungle. So off he flew with a military entourage in a chartered MAF Cessna.

They found Jonas and Nimrod in a village of the Asmat and Larry told them it seemed to be the time to return to Sumapero. The officials and Larry then flew to Sumapero to reassure the few natives they found there.

In the spring of 1978, Larry and Shirley looked forward to attending Chip's graduation from Faith Academy in Manila. Then they planned an extended furlough in the U.S., with all three kids in college there. Shirley's asthma had grown progressively worse, making the timing good for a long break. Larry focused on the completion and dedication of the Wosi church, with nearly a thousand believers attending, before they left.

The night before the Raschers' flight home in early May, huddles of Wosi people slept near the airstrip in Manokwari. At dawn, as the pilot readied the plane, there were tearful goodbyes. They knew it would be a long time before *Bapak Pendita* and *Nyona* returned. They knew the trips on the *Mujizat* would not continue long without the active support of a missionary for planning and repairs. Inasawep, a government building foreman and Larry's right-hand man on the Wosi church-building project, tackled Larry with a bear hug as Larry walked toward the plane. He hung on Larry, weeping, as the waiting pilot fumed.

Larry and Shirley wept as well. How long would it be until they could return? Who would love and encourage these people—Jonas, Nimrod, and the Nafaripi?

But their hearts could not withstand, either, the prospect of having all three of their kids a wide ocean away.

They were at TEAM's annual conference in Chicago that summer when Chuck Preston, newly arrived from Irian Jaya, told them of the murders of Jonas and Nimrod at Sumapero, and the kidnapping of their wives and children.

The story had been told by an eight-year-old girl, the niece of Nimrod and Fitalia. She and the three-year-old daughter of Jonas and Johana had been stolen back from their kidnappers as they camped one night.

At eight years of age, the girl neither knew nor conjectured anything of motives. Perhaps the malcontents had wanted the shortwave radio at Sumapero. It was rumored the group's leader wanted Johana, whom he had taken as his wife. Why did they kill these two teachers when they had not killed teachers anywhere else? Did any Nafaripi—Larry and Shirley felt ill with the thought—collaborate, assist? Yet if some had wanted to harm Jonas, why hadn't they done it during the years he was alone with them?

Larry agonized over his part in sending the men to their deaths. Yet he could not bring himself to fault the commander, much as he would have liked. The commander surely believed the area had been stabilized. And perhaps it had—only to be stirred up again. As always they worked with unknowns in Irian Jaya.

In actuality, the sinister visitors had been hiding in the bushes when Chuck Preston came by float plane to check on the people of Sumapero. They told Jonas and Nimrod they would kill Preston if the two let on anything was wrong.

A few days afterward, Jonas and Nimrod were taken to the point on the riverbank where the float plane landed. "We're going to kill you," they were told. "So get on your knees and pray."

The enemies had guns. The Nafaripi could have resisted, but not against guns. And it was not their way for one or two or a few to resist if the village was not in agreement.

The guns would have been a merciful way, but the attackers riddled the two slight men with arrows. They probably had little ammunition for their stolen guns— if any—and were saving it. Jonas, said the little girl, did not die immediately of his wounds, so he was finished off with an axe.

Both Johana and Fitalia were kidnapped as wives. The mind-set of the primitive woman was such that if an enemy took her, she was his wife; what had happened before was history.

The village of Sumapero was empty—the years of a school and a village, a bizarre anomaly in the tribe's largely uneventful and ancient past. Would a church survive in the jungle?

Johana and Fitalia were not heard from again. There were rumors after a few years, however, that both women had borne children and that Fitalia had died. There was rumor, too, of intertribal warfare.

BONDS THAT ENDURE

Larry and Shirley returned to Irian Jaya for one more term in 1982. Their assignment was to be church planters on Biak, where a church had sprung up from visits by the *Mujizat*. They had come full circle from working with Christian Biakers who were government workers in Kokonao, to working alongside a Biaker teacher at Sumapero, to living and working on the island of Biak.

The *Mujizat* had been sold by TEAM, there being no nationals or missionaries in the intervening years to maintain and use it. The field council was enthusiastic about the boat ministry. But the TEAM missionaries in Manokwari were administrators and Bible teachers. For some reason the new owner never claimed the boat, and it rotted on the shore near Manokwari.

Larry and Shirley lived in a comfortable house on the grounds of the British Leprosy Mission in Biak. At the mission they had a new set of neighbors to invite for dinner and Friday game nights.

In the swamps of the south coast, Sumapero was still deserted. The house Larry built had been stripped of its walls and anything useful to natives. From it sprouted vines and jungle saplings. Shirley's big dinner table had been hacked up for firewood.

The work in Biak was rewarding, and the church

grew. Larry also taught at Dani meetings in the high-lands with old friends Tom and Fran Bozeman, and in the churches in Manokwari.

But as Fran Bozeman and other missionary friends heard more and more frequently on the radio SKED, Shirley was having trouble breathing. Her bronchial asthma was much worse in Biak than other places they'd lived in Irian Jaya.

She and Larry had to leave the field in November 1983. At that point they assumed they could never return to live in Irian Jaya. However, the Lord was in control of their lives, so He must have other work for them to do. But what could they do with this call—this unscratchable itch—and this love for the Indonesian people?

They moved to Denver, where Larry served as Rocky Mountain Area Representative for TEAM. They decorated their family room walls with spears, shields, and carvings from Irian Jaya. Larry kept a large aquarium of vividly colored tropical fish. On a table sat two bronzed shoes, one Greg's and one Karen's, found in the house in Sumapero after the accident. Friends had removed the children's belongings, but Shirley had found these two shoes.

They traveled about the area with an ingenious trailer, dubbed "Larry's traveling woodshed," which displayed Irianese artifacts. They talked in churches about the work in Irian Jaya and recruited new mission-aries for TEAM. Shirley received good medical treatment and her health improved.

When they weren't traveling, they held a weekly Bible study in their home with Indonesian students from the University of Colorado. And they took three short-term mission groups to Irian Jaya and to Java.

At the end of the final one, a work project at a Christian camp in Java, Larry and Shirley flew to Biak. They were met at the Biak airport by a tall, blond

TEAM missionary with a sunburned face wearing a short-sleeved cotton shirt, khaki slacks (it was Sunday so he was dressed up), and flip flops. It was not hard to pick Keith out of the bevy of small, dark, uniformed Indonesians at the tiny airport.

At home on that Sunday morning, Terri Rascher, Keith's wife, was preparing breakfast: pancakes spread with peanut butter, papaya, and powdered milk. Their children, six-year-old Karyn, three-year-old Hannah, and two-year-old Greg, were all tow-headed and red-faced from the heat and the sun. Their Irianese neighbors and playmates watched wide-eyed through the window screens as the family ate. Larry and Shirley fulfilled their longings to be a present Grandma and Grandpa.

The home was compact but attractive, open to breezes, spotlessly clean. The cement floor was cool to feet—always bare inside the Indonesian home—and was swept and mopped daily. The focal point of the living room was a huge aquarium filled with bright fish.

Keith and Larry went diving one day to replenish the tank. Larry expounded to Keith his idea as to how church people in Biak could make an income by supplying tropical fish to pet stores in the U.S.

The home was equipped with a microwave oven, a water bed, and their own deep well for pure drinking water. Still, Terri was thin enough—and, although pretty, she looked worn enough—to show that the life was not easy. They were a few months shy of their first furlough in four years. Terri was warm and cheerful with her house-guests, untiring with good meals and small kindnesses. She enjoyed working and chatting in the kitchen with her mother-in-law who knew the life so well.

One morning *Bapak* Rembekwan, the local pastor, rode to the house on his motorcycle. There had been a death in the church family. A young man had taken sick in the night and died. Probably malaria, but no one would ever know. Keith and Larry were asked to conduct the funeral.

Larry and Shirley entered the home of the dead man's parents, to console the mother and the invalid father. At the cemetery up the road the hole was dug, many men helping. The homemade coffin was lowered and the top showered with flower petals. Family and friends encircled the grave. They sang to a guitar. Some chewed betel nut, a narcotic that stains the teeth and mouth orange. Scruffy dogs wandered about. Larry stepped forward, then Keith, to preach briefly in Indonesian. The people were quiet and attentive.

Larry was proud of his son. Keith's was the better sermon, he was sure. More importantly, Larry was proud that Keith lived with the people, worked with them, dove and fished with them, and played tennis with Indonesian officials. "The people know who loves them," Larry said.

Shirley was in heaven being with the children, helping in the kitchen, visiting with Terri's house helpers, and looking with interest through the *tokos* and open markets for favorite products.

Everywhere people remembered Larry and Shirley—warmly. They came seeking them out. One of them was the cook aboard the *Mujizat* who had watched Larry steer through the storm all night.

The whole family flew to Manokwari on a Merapati commercial flight with a few other passengers and a load of squawking chickens. There they visited the house where they'd lived overlooking the bay. Since missionaries traded things around so, they'd see an old lawn mower of theirs at one place, the outboard the boys skied behind at another. They attended Sunday services at the Wosi church. Larry and Shirley greeted old friends at the door, thoroughly happy. They made a tearful visit to an outdoor service of Wosi church people in their village of Beriosi. They later heard the people stayed, singing and praying for Larry and Shirley through the night.

Keith and Larry drove to where Keith had heard Moses lived. They found him; Larry gave Moses money for a cab, plus some extra, and asked him to come over. Moses brought his son Greg and came for dinner wearing a new yellow knit shirt. He was very thin. Larry knew what Moses did not tell. He lived with his wife's people, alienated from other believers. They were very poor, and when he made money he was beholden, in their culture, to give any to this wife's parents that they asked of him.

Moses told Larry he read the Bible daily and prayed with his children, whom he taught about the Lord. He said he had no regrets.

The only thing left of the *Mujizat,* Larry heard, was her name plate in the sand at Manokwari, and he didn't want to see it.

On the return flight to Biak the plane landed briefly on Numfoor. Keith and Terri had cleaned up the Sweatte house there, and had started visiting periodically to hold meetings on the island.

Larry and Shirley disembarked to visit with people standing around at the airstrip at Numfoor. Someone ran to tell Wambrau they were there. At seventy-three, Wambrau was still diving, but not that day. He hobbled to the airstrip on his platter feet in time to grasp the hand of *Bapak* Rascher. He was a very old man with only a couple of teeth. His son was now a pastor in the town of Merauke, and two of his grandchildren were attending Bible school in Saowi. By the time the plane took off there was a large crowd gathered, waving.

Meanwhile, far away in the district of Tarlac in the Philippines, Kathy Rascher North was finishing the day's school lessons at the kitchen table for Lisa and Ian while little Gina sat with them coloring. Kathy was pregnant with their fourth child, so the more conscious of the heat. The house helper came in from the market with fresh shrimp to prepare for dinner. Kathy's husband David was in his home office preparing for a neighborhood Bible study that evening. They had been working hard as church planters, and after three years had nearly mastered the Tagalog language.

In Michigan, Chip Rascher had finished his daily paperwork as an insurance agent and was working on a house he was constructing with Mark Liebert, a college student and the son of Chip's dorm parents in Sentani. Chip and his wife Jan provided a Stateside home each summer for college-age children of missionaries. After work and dinner he and Mark flew Chip's remote-control airplanes in the lot in back of his house with Chip's three sons, Jonathan, Kyle and Logan.

In a nursing home in Grand Rapids, Michigan, D.J. DePree was sleeping. When he had had to quit teaching Sunday school at age ninety-three, it was more traumatic for him than stepping down as Chairman of the Board of the Herman Miller Furniture Company. If shaken, Mr. DePree didn't wake up. But when a visitor quoted a Scripture verse aloud, D.J.'s eyes popped open. He looked at his visitor as if to say "Oh. I thought I was going to heaven, but it's only you."

In the spring of 1990, Chip paid to bring Moses to Michigan for a few months, to help Chip build houses. But he discovered Moses was no longer well or strong enough to work much. Chip suspected tuberculosis. Mr. DePree asked to see Moses.

Placing his hand on Moses' shoulder, Mr. DePree questioned the fellow to be sure he was a believer. Satisfied, he said, "Young man, I will pray for you the rest of my life."

SO BE IT

By fall of 1990, Larry and Shirley were in their mid-fifties and in need of a change, a challenge. Perhaps Larry was tired of talking to churches about things he wanted to be off doing. The Indonesian Bible study group was thriving, but it whetted their appetites for life with Indonesians. They had bought a camper, but that didn't really help. Larry kept working on the house: landscaping, fixing up the basement, running pipes through the living room wall for his aquarium filter in the garage. They needed to go, to move, to do. They had been in one place far too long, and still sensed this haunting call.

They had discovered on their last short-term mission trip to Indonesia that Shirley's latest asthma medication seemed to work well. But she fared better in Java than in Irian Jaya.

In December they flew to Jakarta, the capital of Indonesia on the island of Java. Their intent was to apply for visas, look for housing, and size up the possibilities of acting as TEAM–government laisons and of Larry's teaching in the TEAM Bible school.

They returned to the States in January, still awaiting word on visas, which were becoming more and more difficult to procure. The job situation looked favorable. Shirley had fared well, but Larry had had stomach trouble much of the trip.

He entered the hospital for gall bladder surgery. The surgeon found tumors the size of pancakes throughout his abdominal cavity and stitched him back up. Lymphoma.

Months of chemotherapy followed, as Larry weakened, visibly aged, lost his energy and his hair, and was nauseated much of the time. He hung onto a verse in the eighteenth chapter of Exodus: "If you do this thing and God so commands you, then you will be able to endure. . . ." If God wanted him to go through cancer for whatever reason, God would be with him and he could endure it. And he and Shirley endured.

In the summer, Shirley saw a doctor in regard to her chest pains and had heart by-pass surgery.

Their children and grandchildren gathered to them from the corners of the earth. Kathy, David and their four children were due for a furlough from the Philippines. Keith, Terri and their three children came to their surprise; their visas had not been renewed by the Indonesian government. Chip, Jan and their sons were in and out as often as they could come from Michigan.

Larry and Shirley moved out of their home into a rental a few blocks away so they could have rest as they needed it. The younger families set up housekeeping in Larry and Shirley's house. Keith came daily to see Larry, to take him out on errands, on diversions, to see to his needs. Larry had been there when Keith needed him, and now Keith wanted to be there for his dad.

Kathy and Terri shared chores and made sure Grandma and Grandpa had the right doses of grandchildren at the right times. Friends and relatives called, wrote and visited. George Boggs, former MAF pilot in Irian Jaya, wrote to Larry: "I'm sure the Lord still has His hand on you. If you can survive Sumapero!!, cannibals!, head hunters!, ship wrecks!! What is cancer?"

head hunters!, ship wrecks!! What is cancer?"

Cancer is tough. Larry was by nature active, gregarious, somewhat impulsive. He struggled with the days and months of convalescence and of wondering whether the disease would be terminal.

Some days he had a hard time reading his Bible or praying. He felt some guilt over that, until he came to the understanding that God heard his prayers—because He knew the disposition of Larry's heart—before words were even formed in his mind. Larry realized that God loved him and He understood. It was all right.

Larry had lots of time to think. Why did Christians suffer? Why had he and Shirley been through all that they had? He wasn't complaining. But he was sure there must be a different answer than the ones they heard most often.

He still rejected the notion, as he had when Greg and Karen were drowned, that it was so he and Shirley could learn some great lesson or so that there would be a dramatic break-though in their work. Certainly there were things they learned, and there were results. But a loving God had not taken their children for these purposes. That equation was too simple. Rather, after God took the children, He worked through the situation for good.

Larry remembered lying delirious with hepatitis in Pirimapun, his liver swollen to the size of a basketball. A native woman had come to him to admonish him, like a friend of Job. "There must be sin in your life and you must come to terms with it," she had said. Other well-meaning but woefully hurtful people had written such things to Shirley after the accident. Of course the consequences of sin lead to trouble. But sin was not the principle reason why Christians had to endure suffering.

Larry felt he found the answer he sought in II Corinthians 1:3–4:

Praise be to the God and Father of our Lord Jesus Christ, the Father of compassion and the God of all comfort, who comforts us in all our troubles, so that we can comfort those in any trouble with the comfort we ourselves have received from God. (NIV)

The memory of the presence of God that Larry and Shirley had sensed the day and night of the accident would be awesomely real to them the rest of their lives. Through that time, and now through their battles with illness, God comforted and encouraged them in very tangible ways, not the least of which was having their whole far-flung family gathered with them.

God allowed Christians to suffer, Larry decided, so that they could know His comfort, His sufficiency for them through whatever trial; and so that they, in turn, could empathize with and participate in God's comforting of others. He didn't need to have experienced the same particular trial as a brother had in order to be able to comfort him. God's comfort, experienced, could be shared with others in any situation.

Larry and Shirley had long understood that their labors in Irian Jaya were for the Lord's ends. Their disappointments and the work seemingly left undone were His concern. They didn't need to see results; they just needed to be obedient to the call. But God chose during this dark period to bring them comfort by reassuring them that their labors had never been in vain.

Before Keith left Irian Jaya he heard that the Nafaripi had returned to Sumapero. In fact, a Bible school graduate from a neighboring tribe had moved with his family to Sumapero to serve as a school teacher and evangelist. Cal Roesler, still a missionary in the south coast swamps after thirty-some years, helped this man settle in and checked on him periodically. The light of faith had not been extinguished in the jungle. Keith had received these three letters from Sumapero:

Primus Raytu to our friend Keith Rascher,

Greetings in the name of Jesus Christ. With this short letter we your friends and servant want to meet you by way of this letter. Now our family are healthy because of the Lord's protection on all of us. [Four children's names follow; they don't keep track of ages.]

We request that you don't forget to pray for us. We don't forget to pray for our friend Keith. We hope for our friend to come to our church group. And when you come don't forget to bring 10 songbooks and 5 Good News Bibles. This is our "order."

Greetings and prayer with our honor,
Primus

On Friday the 2nd, 11th month, year 1990.

Jeremiah Taomanamo in Sumapero.

For missionary named Keith at Numfoor/Biak. I ask to go to the school for male nurses in Senggo. My name is Jeremiah Taomanamo.

Because in our village many people are dying. They've all come back but there aren't many of them.

If you receive this letter, Keith, you can write a letter back or call the school [by radio].

Keith, you could send a letter to me so that I could see the letter. That's as far as I'm writing. Thank you ahead of time.

I say from my heart, blessings to Keith and your wife and children.

Jeremiah Taomanamo

Pendita Keith in Numboor/Biak,

Greetings in Jesus. I consider this letter very important. Now the situation in Sumapero is good. It's peaceful. We have a teacher who is teaching us about the Lord.

We want to invite Keith to visit our village. We have enlarged the church so we are asking Keith to come quickly. We hope you get this letter and that you come with your family.

The church asks for Keith to come and become the leader of the church. Welcome.

We hope Keith with your family will come. We are longing to meet with him whatever year or whatever month we can meet with him.

We know there are those in Sumapero who do not follow the Lord as their Savior. One of the people here David Taomanamo just accepted the Lord, but he hasn't been baptized yet.

We trust that Keith must come so the name of Jesus that hasn't. . . [undecipherable].

That's all and we close with our prayers.

Titus, the church leader
From the church

Unfortunately, by the time the letters got to Keith, he was preparing to return to the States. But God remembered the Nafaripi and had provided a Christian national eager and equipped to teach and help them.

Keith and Terri grieved for their work and their relationships in Irian Jaya. But as the months passed in Denver, they began to look forward to their new assignment with TEAM as church planters in the Philippines. They would have to move their belongings from Irian Jaya to the Philippines and learn a new language, a new culture; but they were committed to the work of church planting. Moreover, regarding their work in Irian Jaya they had been told by the Indonesian government, "Don't ask again"; they didn't know why. And so they moved on.

Slowly both Larry and Shirley improved in health. They had visitors other than family. In the spring three men visited them from Irian Jaya. TEAM had brought nationals from each of their fields to attend their centennial meeting and celebration in Wheaton, Illinois. These men came to see Larry and Shirley afterward. They brought comforting news.

One was a pastor from Kokonao, the site of Larry and Shirley's first assignment in Irian Jaya. When Larry and Shirley left Kokonao, the church there was comprised entirely of government workers and a single Mimika family. Their efforts there among the Mimika had seemed futile. Now the Kokonao church boasted forty-eight adult members, all Mimikas. That news was good therapy.

Other news came to them from Cal Roesler in the spring of 1991. Fitalia, kidnapped wife of Nimrod (who previously was a teacher killed at Sumapero), had come out of hiding with a handful of malcontents. Evidently this group had been sent out by their leaders to see how they would be received. After so many years, would the government allow them to survive and go about their lives? Larry and Shirley knew that of course they would.

Life was very complicated now for Fitalia. She had been married all the years of hiding and had borne children. Her husband was still in hiding with the children, and he didn't want to give her up. Fitalia's relatives wanted and expected her to come home to Amar, where they most likely had a suitable husband picked out for her.

In the fall of 1991, Larry was well enough to camp in the high mesas of northwestern Colorado for hunting with a pastor friend. He was as excited as a kid preparing to go.

While he was gone, Shirley received a call from Jakarta. The visas had been approved—visas which they had applied for a year earlier and had all but forgotten. They must come to Jakarta and receive them by December 24th or lose them.

Again TEAM didn't know what to do with Larry and Shirley Rascher. They wanted to return to Indonesia, but they couldn't possibly be well enough. Larry and Shirley took a detour on a trip to Michigan to meet face-to-face with the heads of TEAM in Wheaton.

They wanted to go to Indonesia to receive the visas. If they received the visas, they reasoned, they could shortly leave the country again on a medical leave. But with the visas, they would have the freedom to go back to settle and work in Jakarta if their health allowed.

And if one of them died there? So be it. After all, there were no guarantees on the length of their lives, regardless of whether they lived in Jakarta or in Denver.

Larry hoped to teach in the Bible school in Jakarta. He wanted to equip nationals to plant churches, and to develop a ministry of evangelism. He wanted to get out into the city with the students, to model how the work could be done. If need be, he could also serve as a laison between TEAM and the Indonesian government.

TEAM gave its blessing, if their supporting churches were behind them. So they went on from Wheaton to Michigan. There the group of small churches who had been proud to have Larry and Shirley as their missionaries since 1961 continued to give their usual support—and more. Larry preached in the churches, and they enjoyed breakfasts, lunches, and dinners out and in homes with old friends.

For Thanksgiving they were in Chip and Jan's home, with Kathy and David's family joining them. Keith and Terri were already in the Philippines, but they talked on the phone. Keith razzed Larry about Denver Bronco football.

Each of their children was safe and happy, with a family of his or her own, and each was serving the Lord. This made Larry and Shirley happy also—but they were restless. Their work for the Lord was unfinished. Somewhere in their heads pounded that incessant drumbeat.

Larry and Shirley flew "home" to Indonesia in December 1991.

This book is dedicated to the glory of God and to the memory of a man who, like Paul, heard the call of God and followed faithfully and obediently to the end. Larry Rascher passed into the presence of his Lord on Friday November 6, 1992.

This book was produced by the Christian Literature Crusade. We hope it has been helpful to you in living the Christian life. CLC is a literature mission with ministry in over 45 countries worldwide. If you would like to know more about us, or are interested in opportunities to serve with a faith mission, we invite you to write to:

Christian Literature Crusade
P.O.Box 1449
Fort Washington, PA 19034